The 4 Attachment Styles in Love

Short Stories Depicting the Challenges of Each Attachment Style in Romantic Relationships

Christine Chin-Sim, Ph.D.

Book Description

"The 4 Attachment Styles in Love" offers an intimate exploration of romantic relationships through a collection of short stories that delve into the complexities of human attachment.

This poignant book delves into the distinct challenges posed by each attachment style: from the yearning of anxious lovers to the guardedness of avoidant souls, from the turmoil of the fearful-avoidant to the steadfastness of the secure, these captivating vignettes reveal the raw emotions and universal struggles that shape our connections with others.

As readers immerse themselves in the rich tapestry of emotions portrayed in these tales, they will find resonance with their own experiences and gain profound insights into the delicate dance of love and attachment.

Dedication

This book is dedicated to my Lord and Savior Jesus Christ. Without Him, I can do nothing. With Him, I can do ALL things as He continues to strengthen me. (Philippians 4:13)

COPYRIGHT

Leverage4change Coaching & Consulting, LLC
Savannah, Georgia

Copyright @ August, 2023 by Leverage4change Coaching & Consulting, LLC

Copyright @ August, 2023 by Christine Chin-Sim, Ph.D.
All rights reserved. No part of this book may be reproduced in any form without written permission from the author.

Introduction

In the tapestry of human emotions and relationships, love stands as both a beacon of joy and a labyrinth of complexities. It's a force that has shaped art, literature, and the very essence of our existence. Yet, for all its splendor, love often comes entwined with a web of emotions, experiences, challenges, with the added complexities of attachment styles formed early in childhood, that can profoundly impact our connections.

Welcome to "The 4 Attachment Styles in Love," a journey into the intricate landscapes of human attachment and the profound influence it exerts upon our romantic relationships. This book is an exploration of the patterns that weave through the fabric of our interactions, shaping our desires, vulnerabilities, challenges, and the ways we interact with others.

At its core, this book seeks to unravel the enigma of attachment styles — the distinct blueprints that guide how we connect with those we hold dear. These styles, born from our earliest experiences and carried into adulthood, serve as the foundation upon which our relationships are built. By understanding and recognizing these styles, we gain a vital key to unlocking deeper self-awareness, that will assist in transforming the dynamics of our partnerships.

My purpose here is twofold: to illuminate the fascinating intricacies of the four primary attachment styles — Secure, Anxious, Avoidant, and Disorganized — and to empower you the reader, with the insights and tools necessary to navigate the labyrinth of love more consciously and harmoniously.

Whether you're seeking to enhance an existing relationship, find solace in self-discovery, or pave the way for more fulfilling future connections, this book endeavors to provide you with a compass for your journey.

As we embark on this exploration, prepare to delve into the stories of fictitious individuals, each representing a distinct attachment style. Through their experiences, you'll glimpse the inner workings of these styles and witness the transformative power that comes from understanding and adopting new ways of managing them. Along the way, you'll uncover practical strategies to foster healthier relationships, navigate conflicts, and nurture the bonds that resonate with your truest self.

But this is not just a book about theories and psychological concepts. In fact, I've chosen to write it in such a way that it can be easily understood and adopted into a new way of being in relationships. It's a testament to the resilience of the human heart, a guide to embracing vulnerability, and a roadmap to shaping the narratives of our emotional lives. As you turn the pages ahead, be open to the revelations that await you — insights that may reshape the way you perceive love, attachment, and the boundless potential for growth that lies within.

So, let us embark together on a voyage through the landscapes of attachment, a voyage that promises not only to unravel the mysteries of our emotional connections but to empower us to forge deeper, more meaningful bonds. The journey may be profound, but the destination — a realm of enriched relationships, profound understanding, and greater self-compassion — is well worth the exploration.

Table of Contents

Book Description 2
Dedication 3
Introduction 5

TRAITS | ANXIOUS PREOCCUPIED ATTACHMENT STYLE 10

TRAITS | FEARFUL AVOIDANT ATTACHMENT STYLE 11

TRAITS | DISMISSIVE AVOIDANT ATTACHMENT STYLE 12

TRAITS | SECURE ATTACHMENT STYLE 13

SIMON'S JOURNEY | DISMISSIVE AVOIDANT ATTACHMENT 14

Chapter 1 | The Roots of Detachment 15
Chapter 2 | The Reluctant Romantic 18
Chapter 3: Love at First Dismissal 21
Chapter 4: The Elusive Commitment 24
Chapter 5 | The Dance of Distance and Closeness 27
Chapter 6 | Unveiling the Past 30
Chapter 7: The Temptation of Freedom 33
Chapter 8 | Facing His Fears 36
Chapter 9 | Choosing Vulnerability 39
Chapter 10: Embracing Love and Growth 42

ELSA – THE FEARFUL AVOIDANT (DISORGANIZED ATTACHMENT) 45

Chapter 1 | Roots of Fearful Avoidance 46
Chapter 2 | The Elusive Connection 50
Chapter 3 | The Battle Within 54
Chapter 4 | The Impact on Career 57
Chapter 5 | Recognizing the Patterns 59
Chapter 6: Unraveling Barriers 61
Chapter 7 | The Impact on Partners 64
Chapter 8 | Breaking Free from Old Patterns 66
Chapter 9 | Embracing Change Through Emotional Intimacy 68
Chapter 10 | Finding Hope and Acceptance 71

CASSIE | THE ANXIOUS PREOCCUPIED ATTACHMENT 74

Chapter 1 | The Roots of Anxious Attachment 75
Chapter 2 | Love's First Whirlwind 81

CHAPTER 3: NEED FOR EMOTIONAL ASSURANCE	87
CHAPTER 4: THE BALANCING ACT	89
CHAPTER 5 ǀ SEEKING SOLACE IN RELATIONSHIPS	92
CHAPTER 6 ǀ UNRAVELING EMOTIONAL DEPENDENCE AND BOUNDARIES	94
CHAPTER 7 ǀ STRENGTHENING COMMUNICATION	97
CHAPTER 8 ǀ A JOURNEY TOWARDS SECURE CONNECTIONS	99
CHAPTER 9 ǀ UNRAVELING OF THREADS	103

[**CELESTE ǀ THE SECURELY ATTACHED**](#) **106**

CHAPTER 1 ǀ THE SECURE FOUNDATION	107
CHAPTER 2 ǀ EMBRACING VULNERABILITY	111
CHAPTER 3 ǀ NURTURING EMOTIONAL INTIMACY	114
CHAPTER 4 ǀ BUILDING TRUST AND SECURITY	117
CHAPTER 5 ǀ EMBRACING & CELEBRATING INDIVIDUALITY	120
CHAPTER 6 ǀ CONFLICT RESOLUTION WITH COMPASSION	123
CHAPTER 7 ǀ SAVORING THE PRESENT MOMENT	126
CHAPTER 8 ǀ NAVIGATING CHANGE AND GROWTH	129
CHAPTER 9 ǀ CELEBRATING LOVE AND CONNECTION	132
CHAPTER 10 ǀ A LOVE THAT ENDURES	135

[**CONCLUSION**](#) **138**

[**AS WE CONCLUDE THIS EXPLORATION INTO THE INTRICATE DANCE OF LOVE AND ATTACHMENT, I HOPE YOU HAVE FOUND A DEEPER UNDERSTANDING OF NOT ONLY THE FOUR ATTACHMENT STYLES THAT SHAPE OUR RELATIONSHIPS BUT ALSO THE BEAUTIFUL COMPLEXITY OF HUMAN EMOTIONS AND CHALLENGES. THROUGH THESE PAGES, WE HAVE DELVED INTO THE PATTERNS THAT GOVERN OUR INTIMATE CONNECTIONS, UNEARTHING THE ROOTS OF OUR DESIRES, FEARS, AND HOPES; AND HOW THEY ARE CONNECTED TO THE EARLY YEARS OF CHILDHOOD.**](#) **138**

Traits | Anxious Preoccupied Attachment Style

- I often worry that my partner doesn't really love me.
- I need a lot of reassurance and validation from my partner to feel secure.
- I tend to overthink and analyze my relationships.
- I feel anxious if my partner doesn't respond to my messages quickly.
- I often feel insecure about my partner's feelings for me.
- I am uncomfortable when my partner wants space or time alone.
- I fear being abandoned or left by my partner.
- I often put my partner's needs above my own, even if it's not reciprocated.
- I tend to jump into relationships and try to move them forward quickly to avoid feeling alone.
- I find it challenging to relax and enjoy a relationship without worrying about its future.

Traits | Fearful Avoidant Attachment Style

- I have difficulty trusting others completely.
- I tend to push people away when they get too close to me emotionally.
- I often feel torn between wanting intimacy and fearing it.
- I avoid getting too attached to avoid getting hurt.
- I am afraid of getting rejected or abandoned in relationships.
- I find it difficult to fully open up and share my feelings with others.
- I tend to have unpredictable mood swings in relationships.
- I fear being vulnerable and letting others see my true self.
- I have experienced a pattern of intense, but short-lived relationships.
- I often feel overwhelmed by the emotional demands of relationships.

Traits | Dismissive Avoidant Attachment Style

- I value my independence and prefer to handle things on my own.
- I find it easy to be alone and don't often feel the need for close relationships.
- I tend to downplay the importance of emotional intimacy.
- I am uncomfortable when others try to get too close or dependent on me.
- I am often seen as distant, cold or uninterested in forming deep connections.
- I prefer not to share my personal problems or emotions with others.
- I am more focused on my own goals and pursuits than on relationships.
- I feel suffocated when my partner becomes too emotionally demanding.
- I am quick to dismiss relationship problems or conflicts as unimportant.
- I have a history of ending relationships without much emotional distress.

Traits | Secure Attachment Style

- I feel comfortable being close and emotionally open in relationships.
- I trust that my partner cares about me and has my best interests at heart.
- I can handle both independence and intimacy in a balanced way.
- I am able to communicate my needs and feelings effectively.
- I don't get overly anxious when my partner needs some space.
- I am supportive of my partner's personal growth and independence.
- I believe that I am worthy of love and respect in a relationship.
- I handle conflicts in a constructive and respectful manner.
- I am generally at ease in most social situations.
- I have healthy and fulfilling long-term relationships.

Remember that attachment styles are complex and can vary based on different factors. Every individual is different and their attachments style is always along a continuum. Their primary traits decide their unconscious ways of operating in relationships, and determines their attachment styles.

These questions are meant to provide some insight, but a comprehensive assessment would involve a deeper exploration of an individual's experiences, behaviors, and beliefs in relationships. If you suspect that attachment issues are affecting your well-being, it might be helpful to discuss your concerns with a therapist.

SIMON'S JOURNEY | DISMISSIVE AVOIDANT ATTACHMENT

Chapter 1 | The Roots of Detachment

Simon's early years were marked by an environment of emotional detachment and self-reliance. Growing up in a household with parents who were often emotionally distant, he learned at a tender age that expressing emotions was not only discouraged but seen as a sign of weakness. This dynamic helped shape the foundation of his dismissive avoidant attachment style.

His father, a stoic and reserved man, believed in the virtues of self-sufficiency and rarely showed affection or empathy towards Simon. Whenever Simon sought comfort or understanding, he was met with dismissive responses like, "You'll be fine," or "Stop crying, it's not a big deal." This constant invalidation taught Simon that his feelings were inconsequential and unworthy of attention.

His mother, on the other hand, was caring but emotionally overwhelmed. She struggled with her own unresolved issues, making it challenging for her to be fully present for Simon. As a result, she often unintentionally reinforced his belief that emotional needs were burdensome and best left unexpressed.

Throughout his childhood, Simon became adept at hiding his feelings. He would retreat to the safety of his room, creating an emotional fortress where no one could penetrate his true emotions.

As the years passed, Simon's dismissive avoidant attachment style became deeply ingrained in his personality. The emotional walls he had erected in his formative years now seemed impenetrable, making it difficult for him to foster meaningful connections and intimate relationships.

Simon also believed that because he was able to take care of his own emotional distress, that others should be able to do the same. As a result, he found others who needed to be "coddled" to be weak, and felt disdain for anyone who needed others to soothe or comfort them during difficult times.

This chapter of Simon's life lays bare the roots of his dismissive avoidant attachment style. It is a poignant reminder of how early experiences can profoundly impact one's emotional development and shape the way they navigate relationships.

As we journey further into Simon's story, we'll witness his struggles and triumphs in unraveling the walls he built within, as he seeks to find a path towards emotional growth and genuine connections with others.

As the years passed, Simon's dismissive avoidant attachment style became deeply ingrained in his personality. The emotional walls he had erected in his formative years now seemed impenetrable, making it difficult for him to foster meaningful connections and intimate relationships.

Simon also believed that because he was able to take care of his own emotional distress, that others should be able to do the same. As a result, he found others who needed to be "coddled" to be weak, and felt disdain for anyone who needed others to soothe or comfort them during difficult times.

This chapter of Simon's life lays bare the roots of his dismissive avoidant attachment style. It is a poignant reminder of how early experiences can profoundly impact one's emotional development and shape the way they navigate relationships.

As we journey further into Simon's story, we'll witness his struggles and triumphs in unraveling the walls he built within, as he seeks to find a path towards emotional growth and genuine connections with others.

Chapter 2 | The Reluctant Romantic

As Simon ventures into the world of romantic relationships, we witness how his dismissive avoidant traits hinder him from fully embracing emotional intimacy. He keeps potential partners at arm's length, afraid of vulnerability and emotional dependence. His partners would complain that there is always this "invisible wall" between them; a point beyond which they knew they were not welcome to tread.

Simon's heart fluttered with nervous excitement as he stepped into the world of romantic relationships. The allure of companionship and the prospect of finding someone to share his life with, beckoned him forward. Yet, underneath the surface, a subtle but powerful force held him back.

He met Sarah at a friend's gathering, and there was an instant spark between them. She was warm, outgoing, and radiated genuine interest in getting to know him. Simon found himself drawn to her charisma and charm, but as their interactions deepened, so did his unease. Whenever Sarah tried to broach topics that delved into emotions or personal vulnerabilities, Simon skillfully steered the conversation towards safer waters.

Afraid of emotional intimacy, he kept potential partners like Sarah at arm's length. He reveled in the initial stages of getting to know someone, but hesitated to cross the threshold of true emotional connection. Like a graceful dancer, he moved gracefully between witty banter and friendly discussions, but when emotions came to the fore, he instinctively withdrew.

Simon's dismissive avoidant traits were a double-edged sword. While they shielded him from emotional turmoil, they also stifled the possibility of genuine connection and intimacy. He believed that leaning on someone emotionally would make him weak and dependent, an outcome he desperately wanted to avoid.

As their relationship progressed, Sarah's affectionate nature clashed with Simon's emotional distance. Frustration brewed between them, and Sarah couldn't understand why Simon was so hesitant to share his feelings or allow her into his inner world. She tried to reassure him that vulnerability was a natural part of being human, but Simon's attachment style had already woven an intricate web around his heart.

His inner dialogue wrestled with conflicting thoughts. On one hand, he yearned for love and intimacy; on the other, he feared the potential emotional turbulence that accompanied such connections. Simon couldn't shake the memories of his childhood, where emotional needs were deemed inconvenient and vulnerable displays were met with disapproval and criticism.

As their relationship faced its first real challenge, Simon's dismissive tendencies intensified. He created distance, both emotionally and physically, using work and other commitments as excuses to avoid confronting the growing emotional tension. Sarah, sensing his detachment, tried to be patient, but her heart yearned for the emotional closeness she craved, and finally made the choice to end the relationship.

In his more reflective moments, Simon recognized the pattern he was caught in. He knew that his dismissive avoidant traits hindered him from experiencing the depth of love and connection he desired. Yet, breaking free from the emotional armor he had built around himself seemed like an insurmountable task.

As Simon continued his journey as "the reluctant romantic," he faced the choice of either embracing emotional intimacy, acknowledging the vulnerabilities within himself, or continuing to let his attachment style dictate the course of his relationships.

The path ahead was uncertain, but Simon's heart knew that confronting his fears was the only way to truly find the love and connection he craved – a love that would transcend the barriers of his dismissive avoidant traits and touch the core of his being.

Chapter 3 | Love at First Dismissal

Enter Jennifer, a compassionate and understanding woman who falls for Simon's charm, but struggles to break down his emotional walls. We explore how Simon grapples with his inner conflicts when confronted with Jennifer's emotional openness.

Jennifer entered Simon's life like a gentle breeze, carrying with her an aura of warmth and understanding. She was a woman who embraced her emotions and wore her heart on her sleeve. From their very first meeting, she felt a connection with Simon, drawn to his intelligence and wit, coupled with a sense of mystery.

Simon, too, couldn't help but be captivated by Jennifer's kindness and emotional openness. He admired her ability to express herself freely and envied the ease with which she navigated the world of emotions. He silently wished he was able to express himself so freely, but didn't know where to begin. As their friendship blossomed into something deeper, Simon found himself grappling with his inner conflicts.

He was constantly torn between the longing to embrace Jennifer's affection and the instinct to pull away to maintain emotional distance. A part of him yearned for the emotional intimacy Jennifer offered, but another part feared the vulnerability that came with it. The walls he had constructed around his heart were sturdy, and he feared that letting Jennifer in might expose him to emotional turbulence.

As they spent more time together, Jennifer sensed Simon's emotional guardedness. She tried to create a safe space for him to open up, sharing her own vulnerabilities and feelings, and hoping he would reciprocate. But each time she approached the subject of emotions or tried to encourage deeper conversations, Simon found ways to deflect or change the topic.

In the rare moments when Simon allowed himself to be vulnerable, he felt an unsettling mix of relief and discomfort. He was unaccustomed to the exposure of his emotions and found himself questioning whether he was overreacting or being too sensitive. This inner turmoil was a manifestation of his dismissive avoidant attachment style, causing him to question the validity of his own feelings.

Jennifer's patience and empathy were unwavering. She could sense the internal struggle Simon was facing, recognizing that his emotional defenses were not a reflection of his true feelings for her. Instead of pushing him to change or trying to "fix" him, Jennifer offered a steady presence and a listening ear, allowing Simon the time and space to navigate his emotions at his own pace.

Their relationship was a dance of contradictions – moments of genuine connection interspersed with periods of emotional distance. Jennifer knew that breaking down Simon's emotional walls would require patience and understanding, but she was willing to invest in their love, hoping that one day Simon would feel safe enough to embrace emotional intimacy.

Simon's inner conflicts were lessened as a result of Jennifer's patience and resolve to stick things through. However, being with Jennifer challenged him to confront his dismissive avoidant tendencies and he began to question the validity of the emotional fortress he had built around himself. Through her actions, Jennifer taught him that vulnerability was not synonymous with weakness, and emotional intimacy was not a threat but a gift of deeper connection.

As the relationship deepened, Simon's attachment style clashed with the love he felt for Jennifer. He had to make a choice – to continue hiding behind his emotional defenses and risk losing a chance at love or to step outside his comfort zone and allow himself to be vulnerable, embracing the emotional connection he had long resisted.

The journey ahead was uncertain, and Simon knew that confronting his inner conflicts would be daunting. But in the presence of Jennifer's unwavering love and understanding, he felt a glimmer of hope that he could navigate through the labyrinth of his dismissive avoidant attachment and find the courage to let love in.

Chapter 4 | The Elusive Commitment

In this chapter, we see Simon's ambivalence towards commitment. While he enjoys the companionship, and despite Jennifer's unwavering commitment, he becomes restless when the relationship starts feeling too emotionally demanding. His dismissive avoidant traits led to a fear of being trapped, causing turmoil in the relationship.

Soon, a new challenge emerged - the question of commitment. While Simon enjoyed the companionship and connection they shared, he couldn't shake the growing restlessness within him. His dismissive avoidant attachment style was pushing him to maintain emotional distance, fearing the perceived entrapment that commitment might bring.

With every milestone in their relationship, whether it was spending more time together or discussing future plans, Simon's internal turmoil intensified. He loved Jennifer's company, but the idea of committing to a long-term relationship ignited a sense of unease in him. The fear of emotional dependence and losing his sense of independence, began to overshadow the love he had for her.

Simon found himself pulling away whenever the topic of commitment arose. He'd offer vague responses, change the subject altogether, or asks, why the hurry? After all, weren't they happy just the way they are?

He would constantly evade any conversation that Jennifer earnestly tried to initiate regarding moving forward to the next stage of commitment. She would notice his discomfort but hesitated to confront him about it, worried that addressing the issue might push him further away.

His dismissive avoidant traits were a double-edged sword - they granted him the freedom to maintain emotional autonomy but hindered him from fully embracing the depth of emotional connection that comes with commitment. He yearned for the sense of security and comfort that commitment could offer, yet he was afraid of relinquishing the control he felt with his emotional walls intact. This tug-of-war between his desire for emotional intimacy and his fear of being trapped, sent ripples of turmoil through their relationship.

Jennifer, who was emotionally invested and committed to their bond, struggled to understand Simon's hesitation. She knew he cared for her, but she couldn't comprehend why he couldn't fully embrace their love and commit to a shared future.

Simon's inner conflict led to moments of distance between them. He'd withdraw, seeking solace in solitude, to gather his thoughts and emotions; leaving Jennifer feeling confused and insecure about their relationship. The emotional push-and-pull frustrated her, making her wonder if she could truly have a future with someone who seemed perpetually on the fence about commitment.

As they navigated this tumultuous chapter, Simon was faced with a choice - to confront his dismissive avoidant traits and push past his fear of commitment or to continue retreating into emotional detachment, risking the loss of a meaningful connection with Jennifer.

The journey ahead was uncertain, and Simon grappled with the conflicting desires within him. He knew that for their relationship to thrive, he would need to challenge his attachment style and open himself up to the vulnerability that comes with commitment. But taking that leap meant breaking down the walls he had so carefully constructed, exposing himself to the discomfort of emotional intimacy.

Simon's ambivalence towards commitment serves as a pivotal moment in their relationship. It became evident that his dismissive avoidant traits were not only affecting his emotional well-being, but also the connection he shared with Jennifer.

The question that lingers is whether Simon can find the courage to confront his fears and embrace the emotional depth of commitment, or whether the elusive pull of emotional distance will dictate the course of their love story.

Chapter 5 | The Dance of Distance and Closeness

As Simon oscillates between seeking and avoiding intimacy with Jennifer, their relationship faces many challenges. Simon's struggle with expressing affection and vulnerability creates a sense of isolation and distance that affects their emotional bond.

Their relationship had always been a delicate dance, a delicate interplay of distance and closeness. At times, they seemed inseparable, their laughter and affection filling the air like a warm breeze. But just as quickly, Simon would withdraw, retreating behind his emotional walls, leaving Jennifer feeling like she was grasping at thin air.

The pattern of isolation and uncertainty in their relationship began to take its toll on both of them. Simon's dismissive avoidant attachment style was the driving force behind this emotional dance. He struggled with expressing affection and vulnerability, and his instinct to retreat whenever emotions ran deep only intensified their emotional turmoil.

During moments of intimacy, Simon allowed himself to be vulnerable, and their connection would soar to heights that made both of their hearts sing. But as the emotional intensity increased, so did Simon's discomfort. Fearing the perceived loss of control and independence, he'd instinctively pull back, creating a chasm between them.

Jennifer couldn't help but feel hurt and confused by Simon's inconsistent behavior. She'd experience moments of immense closeness, only to be followed by periods of emotional distance that left her questioning the authenticity of their connection. The uncertainty of not knowing where she stood with him gnawed at her heart.

Simon loved Jennifer deeply, but his dismissive avoidant traits made it difficult for him to fully embrace emotional intimacy. His emotional walls were a fortress that protected him from potential hurt, but they also served as barriers that prevented him from fully experiencing the depth of love and connection that Jennifer offered.

As the pattern continued, Jennifer tried to confront Simon about his emotional withdrawal, hoping to understand his feelings and thoughts. But Simon, ever the master of evasion, would deflect or downplay his actions, leaving her feeling unheard and invalidated. He knew that if he continued on this path, he risked losing the love and connection he cherished with Jennifer.

In his quieter moments, Simon reflected on the reasons behind his emotional defenses. Determined to break the cycle, Simon decided to seek professional help. Therapy became a safe space for him to explore his emotions, confront his fears, and learn healthier ways to communicate and connect with Jennifer. With time and effort, he began to let down his emotional barriers, slowly allowing Jennifer to see the vulnerable and authentic side of him.

As Simon took steps towards emotional growth, the dance of distance and closeness began to change its tempo. The periods of emotional distance became less frequent, and moments of genuine intimacy and connection became more sustained. Jennifer, in turn, appreciated Simon's efforts and the progress he was making, giving them both hope for a stronger and more secure emotional bond.

Simon's struggle with expressing affection and vulnerability creates turbulence in their relationship. However, through introspection and the determination to confront his dismissive avoidant attachment style, he takes the first steps towards breaking free from this toxic pattern. Their journey towards emotional growth and deeper connection sets the stage for the transformative chapters that lie ahead in their love story.

Chapter 6 | Unveiling the Past

As Simon delves deeper into his journey of self-discovery, he knew that understanding the roots of his dismissive avoidant attachment style was crucial. Through introspection and encounters with his past, he began to peel back the layers that shrouded his emotional defenses with the help and guidance from his therapist.

Therapy became a crucial tool in this process, providing a safe and non-judgmental space for Simon to explore his inner world. Guided by a compassionate therapist, he revisited pivotal moments from his childhood, seeking to unravel the origins of his emotional barriers.

One of the earliest memories that surfaced during therapy was from when Simon was just a young child. He recalled a moment of vulnerability when he sought comfort from his father after a particularly difficult day at school. Instead of embracing him with understanding, his father brushed off his feelings, chiding him to "toughen up" and not let the world get to him. In that moment, Simon learned that expressing emotions was undesirable and that seeking emotional support could lead to rejection.

Another significant event etched in Simon's memory was the divorce of his parents. Witnessing the breakdown of their relationship left him feeling adrift and alone, further solidifying his belief that relying on others emotionally was a precarious endeavor. He soon learned to suppress his feelings and rely solely on himself as a way to cope with the emotional upheaval.

Simon's introspection also led him to explore his relationship with his mother. While she was caring, she struggled to provide the emotional support he needed, often preoccupied with her own challenges. This left Simon feeling emotionally neglected and reinforced his belief that seeking emotional connection was futile.

As these memories resurfaced, Simon's therapist helped him to connect the dots between his childhood experiences and his dismissive avoidant attachment style. He realized that his emotional defenses were not an inherent part of his personality, but rather a response to the emotional landscape of his formative years.

Throughout the therapy sessions, Simon grappled with mixed emotions. He felt anger and sadness for the emotional neglect he experienced, but he also felt a sense of empathy and understanding towards his parents, recognizing that they, too, had their struggles and limitations.

As he allowed his past to be unveiled, Simon gained newfound clarity about how his childhood shaped his emotional coping mechanisms. He understood that the dismissive avoidant attachment style was a survival strategy he had developed as a means to protect himself from potential hurt and rejection. But now, armed with this knowledge, he knew he had the power to rewrite his emotional script and find healthier ways to connect with others.

With the support of his therapist, Simon began to challenge the beliefs that had held him captive for so long. He learned to embrace vulnerability and express his feelings, gradually dismantling the emotional walls he had erected around his heart.

As Simon journeyed through the chapters of his past, he discovered a profound sense of self-compassion. He acknowledged that his emotional defenses had served a purpose, protecting him during times of vulnerability. But now, as he embarked on a path of healing, he realized that the time had come to let go of those defenses and create new patterns of emotional connection.

Unveiling the past was not an easy or comfortable process for Simon, but it was an essential one. Simon now knew that understanding the roots of his dismissive avoidant attachment style was the key to fostering healthier and more fulfilling relationships, not only with Jennifer but with himself as well.

As Simon continued his journey of self-discovery, he felt a newfound sense of hope and empowerment, knowing that he held the pen to rewrite the narrative of his story.

Chapter 7 | The Temptation of Freedom

In the midst of Simon's journey towards emotional growth and healing, an unexpected encounter stirred the waters of his heart. Maya, a free-spirited artist, entered his life like a whirlwind of color and spontaneity. Her carefree nature and adventurous spirit stood in stark contrast to Simon's cautious demeanor, and he found himself drawn to her magnetic energy.

As Simon and Maya crossed paths, he felt an exhilarating sense of freedom that had been absent from his life for far too long, and somehow saw Jennifer's need for commitment as a threat to the spontaneity Maya offered. Maya's spontaneity seemed like a breath of fresh air, a departure from the emotional entanglements he had been navigating with Jennifer. He was entranced by the idea of escaping the complexities of emotional intimacy and embracing a life of carefree abandon. Deep within himself, he knew this was just an excuse to not having to deal with the challenges of change; but he ignored the warnings.

Maya's infectious laughter and zest for life, became an alluring escape for Simon. Her presence offered a temporary reprieve from the emotional work he had been engaging in with Jennifer. In Maya's company, he could momentarily forget the tangled web of feelings and uncertainties that had become synonymous with his relationship with Jennifer.

As Simon spent more time with Maya, he found himself captivated by the allure of her world. She encouraged him to embrace spontaneity and let go of his worries, a stark contrast to the emotional introspection he had been undertaking.

He became enamored with the idea of living in the present, free from the emotional complexities that came with committed relationships. Yet, beneath the surface of newfound freedom, a subtle sense of guilt tugged at Simon's heart. He couldn't help but question the motives behind his attraction to Maya. Was he genuinely drawn to her adventurous spirit, or was she merely an escape from the challenges he faced with Jennifer? He grappled with the conflicting desires within him - the yearning for emotional freedom and the fear of losing the love he had for Jennifer.

As Simon navigated this precarious territory, he knew he had to confront his emotions and be honest with himself. He recognized that Maya represented a temporary escape from the emotional work he needed to do with Jennifer. In her carefree demeanor, he saw a reflection of the parts of himself that he had kept suppressed for so long.

As he wrestled with his feelings, Simon realized that Maya could be a catalyst for his growth, but she couldn't be a substitute for the depth of emotional connection he had with Jennifer. The temptation of freedom was enticing, but he knew deep down that he couldn't run away from his emotional challenges forever.

In a moment of clarity, Simon decided to confront the situation head-on. He opened up to Jennifer about his encounter with Maya, sharing the conflicting emotions he was experiencing. To his surprise, Jennifer, though visibly hurt by his betrayal, responded with understanding and patience, appreciating his honesty and vulnerability, and seeing it as progress on his part.

In their conversation, Simon realized that his attraction to Maya was not a betrayal of his feelings for Jennifer but rather a manifestation of his journey towards healing. He acknowledged that he needed to explore his desire for freedom and spontaneity, without compromising the depth of his emotional connection with Jennifer and causing her much pain.

As he continued to navigate the complexities of his emotions, Simon learned valuable lessons about the importance of being honest with himself and his partner. He discovered that true emotional freedom came from confronting his fears and embracing vulnerability, rather than seeking escape in the arms of another.

Simon faced the temptation of freedom and the allure of a carefree spirit. But through introspection and the support of Jennifer, he learned that true growth and emotional liberation could only be found by confronting his inner conflicts and embracing the transformative power of emotional intimacy.

The journey ahead was uncertain, but Simon was now armed with newfound understanding and resolve, ready to embrace the challenges that lay ahead in his quest for emotional healing and authentic connection.

Chapter 8 | Facing His Fears

Simon decided to end his affair with Maya and knew it was time to confront his emotional limitations head-on. As he reflected on his feelings for Maya, he recognized that his attraction to her was not a genuine romantic connection but a reflection of the freedom he had longed for. With honesty and compassion, he had a heart-to-heart conversation with Maya, explaining his emotional journey and the clarity he had gained. He expressed gratitude for the experiences they shared but knew that their paths would diverge.

His feelings for Jennifer were genuine, and he couldn't bear the thought of losing the connection they shared. And although he couldn't deny the pull of freedom and spontaneity that Maya represented; he knew it was unfair to deliberately hurt Jennifer when she had always stood by him, despite the mistakes of his past.

As he continued to seek guidance from his therapist and through introspection and therapy sessions, he began to explore ways to cultivate emotional intimacy and connection. He learned to sit with uncomfortable emotions, to embrace vulnerability, and to communicate openly with Jennifer about his struggles.

Facing his fears was not an easy process. He grappled with moments of self-doubt and uncertainty, but he knew that true growth came from pushing through the discomfort. He engaged in practices that encouraged emotional expression, such as journaling and mindfulness exercises.

Slowly but surely, he chipped away at the emotional walls that had been imprisoning him for so long. With Jennifer's unwavering support, Simon found the courage to explore the depth of their emotional connection. They engaged in heartfelt conversations about their fears and hopes, their dreams and vulnerabilities. Simon discovered that opening up to Jennifer brought a sense of liberation he had never experienced before. He felt seen and understood in a way that he had always longed for, but never allowed himself to embrace.

In the process of confronting his dismissive avoidant tendencies, Simon realized that the emotional distance he had maintained was not a sign of strength but of self-imposed isolation. He learned that true strength came from vulnerability and the ability to rely on others emotionally. The more he embraced this newfound understanding, the more he felt a sense of empowerment in his relationships.

As the chapters of Simon's life unfolded, he was filled with a sense of liberation he had never known before. The fear of intimacy that had once held him captive was now becoming a distant memory. He had faced his fears head-on, embracing emotional growth and healing.

Simon realized that emotional intimacy was not a trap but a source of strength. The love he shared with Jennifer deepened, and their emotional bond grew stronger than ever before. As he continued to explore the depths of vulnerability and emotional connection, he found himself on a path of growth and transformation.

Simon's journey was far from over, but he now had the tools and understanding to navigate the complexities of love and relationships. He continued to embrace the vulnerability that comes with authentic connections, knowing that it was the key to unlocking the truest form of love and fulfillment in his life.

Chapter 9 | Choosing Vulnerability

Simon's journey of self-discovery and emotional growth continued, was never a linear path. There were "ups and downs and turnarounds" but with the support of Jennifer and the help of his therapist, he persisted. The temptation to retreat into his emotional fortress was still present, a lingering pull towards the familiar safety of emotional detachment. The fear of being hurt and rejected loomed large, reminding him of the comfort he found in keeping others at arm's length. But alongside that fear, a newfound understanding of vulnerability tugged at his heart, beckoning him towards a path of authenticity and emotional depth.

Simon wrestled with his choices, torn between the comfort of his emotional defenses and the yearning for a genuine connection with Jennifer. He knew that embracing vulnerability meant risking emotional exposure and the possibility of getting hurt. But he also recognized that vulnerability was the gateway to the depth of love and intimacy he craved, and every day he had to choose to stay the course of change toward becoming more securely attached.

As he grappled with his inner conflicts, Simon continued to seek guidance from his therapist and leaned on the support of Jennifer. She, too, had been on a journey of understanding and acceptance, and she encouraged Simon to trust in the power of vulnerability.

One evening, during a heartfelt conversation with Jennifer, Simon bared his soul. He laid his emotions bare, sharing his inner struggles and the fear that had held him captive for so long. He expressed his desire to break free from the emotional fortress he had constructed and embrace the discomfort of vulnerability.

Simon made a gigantic step toward his healing, when, in that moment of honesty and vulnerability, something shifted within him. He felt a weight lift off his shoulders, as if releasing years of pent-up emotions. It was the courage to lay his heart on the line, to show his true self to the world, and to accept the possibility of love and connection, even in the face of uncertainty.

Choosing vulnerability was a gradual process, and Simon knew that it wouldn't be without its challenges. He understood that old habits die hard and that retreating into emotional detachment might still be a temptation during difficult times. But he was determined to stay the course, knowing that the path of vulnerability was where true emotional growth and fulfillment lay.

As Simon continued to embrace vulnerability, he witnessed a profound transformation in his relationship. His emotional connection with Jennifer deepened, and their love blossomed into something more beautiful than he had ever imagined. The walls that once separated them crumbled, and they forged a bond built on trust, authenticity, and mutual understanding. While the journey of vulnerability wasn't without its bumps and hurdles, Simon felt a newfound sense of resilience within himself.

Choosing vulnerability had a ripple effect on other aspects of Simon's life as well. In his career, he found the courage to take risks and pursue opportunities that required emotional intelligence – that once seemed unattainable. He embraced vulnerability as a means of growth and self-discovery, knowing that it was through embracing discomfort that he could unlock his full potential.

Simon knew that vulnerability would need to be a lifelong practice. But with each step, he felt a deeper connection to himself, to Jennifer, and to the world around him. Choosing vulnerability was the defining moment that set him on a path of emotional liberation and genuine connection, forever changing the trajectory of his romantic and casual relationships, paving the way for connections that are built on the bedrock of vulnerability and authenticity.

Chapter 10 | Embracing Love and Growth

As Simon continued to embrace vulnerability and delve into the depths of self-awareness, he felt a profound transformation taking place within him. The seeds of emotional growth, nurtured through therapy and introspection, were beginning to bear fruit. He was no longer defined solely by his dismissive avoidant attachment style; instead, he was cultivating healthier attachment patterns that allowed for more fulfilling relationships.

The journey towards healthier attachment patterns was not without its challenges. Simon faced moments of self-doubt and moments of regression, but he refused to let those setbacks deter or define him. With the support of his therapist and the love and understanding of Jennifer, he continued to press forward. He began to understand that his dismissive avoidant tendencies were not fixed personality traits but responses to past experiences. Armed with this awareness, he developed new coping mechanisms that enabled him to navigate emotional intimacy with greater ease.

His newfound self-awareness and emotional resilience propelled him forward in his professional life, leading to a sense of fulfillment and success he had never experienced before. In his romantic relationship with Jennifer, Simon's growth was evident in the depth of their connection. They shared moments of genuine intimacy and emotional closeness that he once thought was beyond his reach.

He no longer feared expressing his feelings or seeking support from Jennifer. Their love blossomed into a partnership built on trust, empathy, and open communication.

As Simon continued to nurture healthier attachment patterns, he also found himself attracting and building more fulfilling romantic relationships outside of his partnership with Jennifer. He was no longer drawn solely to partners who mirrored his dismissive avoidant tendencies, but instead, he sought emotional connection and authenticity in his relationships.

He now felt a newfound sense of hope and acceptance within himself and the emotional fortress he once relied on to protect himself had been replaced by an open heart that embraced the uncertainties and joys of life.

The transformation within Simon was not a final destination but an ongoing journey. He knew that emotional growth was a continuous process, and he remained committed to self-improvement and fostering healthier attachment patterns.

Simon's life has been enriched in immeasurable ways and as he looked back on his journey; Simon felt gratitude for the challenges he had faced, as they had led him to this moment of self-awareness and transformation. He had come to understand that the key to embracing love and growth was acceptance - accepting the past, accepting vulnerability, and accepting himself for who he truly was.

With a newfound sense of hope and acceptance, Simon faced the future with an open heart and an unwavering commitment to continue nurturing healthier attachment patterns. As he embraced love and growth, he knew that the possibilities for connection and fulfillment were limitless, and he was excited to continue writing the next chapters of his life with a renewed sense of purpose and authenticity.

ELSA – THE FEARFUL AVOIDANT (DISORGANIZED ATTACHMENT)

Chapter 1 | Roots of Fearful Avoidance

In the quiet corners of Elsa's mind, memories of her childhood lie dormant, but their echoes continue to reverberate in the patterns of her adult life. As we delve into Elsa's past, we find a tapestry of experiences that shaped her fearful avoidant attachment style.

Elsa's early years were colored by an unpredictable and emotionally volatile environment. Her parents, though loving, struggled with their own emotional and mental baggage, leading to inconsistent displays of affection and support, with an ever-present undertone of chaos and conflict; interspersed with violence.

Her father was an alcoholic, and neither herself or her mother could predict his state of mind he would have when he finally ventured home. On the rare moments her father was sober, he was loving and kind; but these moments were few and far between and were often overshadowed by periods of physical and emotional volatility, and emotional distance. As a young child, Elsa experienced a rollercoaster of emotions, never knowing what to expect from her father or the world around her.

Her mother tried to temper this unpredictability, and to have some type of order in their lives, but she was also fighting a battle of her own, by trying to tiptoe around her husband when he was around. This left Elsa feeling unsafe and unsure of how or when to seek comfort or support from her parents. When she cried or expressed vulnerability, she received mixed responses - sometimes met with nurturing, other times with dismissal or just outright, emotional, verbal, or physical abuse.

Over time, Elsa learned to adapt to this ever-changing emotional landscape and developed a keen sense of the ability to perceive when there was danger, and when to become "invisible" in order not to attract attention to herself. She learned to be self-reliant, keeping her feelings and needs hidden to avoid potential rejection or disappointment; and very soon, her fear of abandonment and rejection took root, leading her to suppress her emotions and desires, in order to shield herself from potential emotional and physical pain.

In order to protect herself, she learned how to read the micro-expressions of those around her, and she knew instinctively, when to approach or when to retreat for her safety. Unfortunately, as she entered adult relationships, this proved to be a double-edged sword, where she frequently mis-read the expressions of others and reacted in ways she learned subconsciously as a child.

As Elsa grew older, these early experiences continued to influence her interactions with others. She found it challenging to trust and rely on others, fearing that they would leave or hurt her, just as she had experienced in her early relationships with her caregivers. This internal struggle between yearning for emotional connection and avoiding potential heartache and pain, created a constant push-and-pull dynamic in her romantic relationships.

Elsa's attachment style was further reinforced by the messages she received from the world around her. Society often valorizes independence and self-sufficiency, reinforcing her belief that displaying vulnerability and needing emotional support were signs of weakness. While deep in her heart, she longed for someone she could depend on to show her the emotional support she was deprived of as a child.

As she stepped into adolescence and young adulthood, Elsa's fearful avoidant attachment style continued to shape her relationships and personal life. She would enter romantic partnerships with a sense of hope, yearning for love and connection, but as the relationship deepened, she couldn't help but pull away, terrified of the vulnerability that came with emotional intimacy.

Because the fearful avoidant attachment is a combination of the anxious and the avoidant styles; this is particularly challenging for Elsa. In relationships with an anxious partner – she finds herself feeling suffocated and restricted because of the clinginess of someone with the anxious attachment style. However, if her partner was avoidant, she transforms into the anxious style, where she now embodies the traits of the anxious individual.

Elsa also struggled in friendships, where she found it difficult to open up and trust others fully, fearing that her true self would be rejected or judged. There was always this underlying, nudging belief, that if anyone knew who she really was, they could not love her. After all, if her own parents could not love her - how could anyone else?

Her professional life also felt the impact of her attachment style, as she hesitated to seek help or guidance from colleagues, preferring to tackle challenges on her own and found it difficult and uncomfortable to perform in team settings.

As Elsa confronts her past and explores her attachment style, she begins to see the potential for growth and healing. Armed with self-awareness, she knows that the journey ahead won't be easy, but she is determined to face her fears and embrace vulnerability.

Chapter 2 | The Elusive Connection

Elsa's struggle to form deep connections with others, especially romantic partners, has been a recurring theme in her life. Her fearful avoidant attachment style, rooted in her childhood experiences, plays a significant role in shaping these challenges.

In her first romantic encounter, Elsa meets Alex, a kind and caring individual who shows genuine interest in getting to know her. At the beginning of their relationship, Elsa is drawn to Alex's warmth and attentiveness, yet she can't help but feel a nagging sense of unease. As their emotional intimacy deepens, Elsa's fear of vulnerability intensifies. She worries that if she allows herself to fully open up to Alex, she might expose her insecurities and be rejected.

In an attempt to protect herself, Elsa starts to withdraw emotionally. She becomes guarded, avoiding discussions about her feelings and pushes Alex away when he attempts to break through her emotional barriers. Alex senses her emotional distance and feels frustrated and confused, unsure of how to bridge the gap between them.

Elsa's fearful avoidant traits continue to impact her relationship with Alex. She oscillates between moments of intense longing for closeness and the impulse to retreat into emotional isolation. This push-and-pull dynamic leaves both Elsa and Alex feeling confused and emotionally unfulfilled.

As their relationship progresses, Elsa's fear of emotional intimacy heightens. The more she cares about Alex, the more she fears the potential pain of losing him. This fear causes her to create emotional distance, believing that if she keeps her feelings at bay, she can protect herself from heartache.

Eventually, the strain becomes too much for Alex, and he shares his concerns with Elsa. He opens up about his desire for a deeper emotional connection and his struggle to understand her emotional withdrawals. Elsa's initial reaction is to distance herself further, afraid that her fears will inevitably lead to rejection.

This confrontation becomes a turning point for Elsa. Although, she realizes that her avoidance of emotional intimacy is not only affecting her but also her partner; she cannot tame the need to flee. And flee she does. She makes excuses to Alex and says she needs some time to figure stuff out. But because she is so desperate for the emotional connection she also fears, she escapes right into the arms of another. But the cycle continues – because unfortunately we cannot run away from our attachment traits; we must confront them in order to heal.

Enter Daniel. He is charismatic and adventurous, and Elsa is initially captivated by his spontaneity. However, her fearful avoidant attachment style resurfaces, causing her to approach the relationship with caution.

Entertaining another love interest, while still in relationship with another, is one way the fearful avoidant self-sabotages relationships. In a weird type of way, by sabotaging their relationship, which usually results in a breakup, it becomes a self-fulfilling prophecy which validates her belief that relationships never last and cannot be trusted.

With Daniel, the pattern continues, and Elsa falls into a familiar pattern of emotional ambivalence. She enjoys their time together but is wary of getting too close. The more Daniel expresses his affection, the more Elsa feels the impulse to retreat. She fears that allowing herself to love and be loved would make her vulnerable to heartbreak.

These encounters with Alex and Daniel reflect the challenges Elsa faces in forming deep connections. Her fear of emotional intimacy creates an internal tug-of-war, leaving her feeling torn between her desire for love and her fear of vulnerability. The emotional distance she creates by entertaining two partners at the same time, relieves some of the tension felt, because a deeper connection is expected with one partner.

As such, the inability to go "all in" with one partner, causes friction in her relationships and becomes a self-fulfilling prophecy, as her fearful avoidant traits prevent her from experiencing the emotional closeness she truly craves.

As Elsa reflects on these encounters, she realizes that her attachment style is a barrier to the intimacy and connection she longs for. She knows that if she wants to break free from this pattern, she must confront her fears and embrace vulnerability. But she needs help. And fast.

She sought out the help of a therapist with experience of the attachment styles, and made an appointment to seek help immediately. Enough was enough.

Chapter 3 | The Battle Within

As Elsa's relationship with Alex remains in limbo, the clash between her fear of emotional intimacy and her desire for a meaningful connection becomes more pronounced. The emotional rollercoaster she experiences is both exhilarating and terrifying, leaving her grappling with moments of intense vulnerability and the impulse to retreat into emotional isolation.

In her period of self-isolation, she reflects on the moments of closeness with Alex, and feels a rush of emotions she had long suppressed. She cherished the tender moments they shared, the laughter, the shared interests, and the genuine affection they exchanged. However, beneath the surface of happiness, a familiar fear lingers - the fear of getting too close, too attached, and the fear of potential heartbreak.

She decides to reconnect with Alex, and for a while, Elsa's guard starts to come down, and she finds herself slowly opening up to Alex. She apologized for the pain she caused him and explained that she was getting help from a therapist. She asks for his patience and help during this time of healing.

Alex, was understanding and welcomes her back into his life. She allows herself to share pieces of her past, her dreams, and her fears, but with each revelation, she feels the impulse to withdraw, fearing that her openness will push Alex away.

The contrast between her desire for a meaningful connection and her fear of vulnerability continues to creates internal turmoil for Elsa. She explains this to Alex and he promised to help her as much as possible.

In her therapy sessions, she battles with her emotions, wanting to take a leap of faith into emotional intimacy, while simultaneously holding herself back, as if instinctively protecting her heart from potential pain. Her therapist was patient and allowed her the space to work through her emotional swings; asking pertinent questions that allowed her to break through her usual pattern of reacting to the thoughts, feelings and emotions that arises.

Moments of intense vulnerability with Alex are bittersweet for Elsa. She feels a sense of liberation in sharing her authentic self, yet it is accompanied by a looming dread of vulnerability. This conflict often leads to emotional turbulence within the relationship, as Alex also senses Elsa's emotional withdrawals and becomes uncertain of how to break through her emotional barriers. But Alex stood his ground, and allowed Elsa the time and space to work through her emotions, while assuring her that he was there for her.

She had never had anyone who didn't give up on her, so she found herself trusting Alex even more. Even when the impulse to retreat into emotional isolation beckons, Elsa is reminded and comforted that Alex was there for her.

Soon, she begins to allow herself to open up more to Alex about her challenges. How isolating herself was a way to shield herself from the perceived dangers of emotional intimacy because she convinces herself that by creating distance, she can protect herself from potential heartache.

Elsa realizes that this internal battle was also very difficult for Alex and expresses her gratitude for his patience with her. As she reflects on the problems in her relationship with Alex, she realizes that her fearful avoidant attachment style is causing her to self-sabotage potential for genuine intimacy. The fear of emotional intimacy, stemming from her past experiences, has become a formidable barrier to the depth of connection she longs for.

In the following chapters of her journey, Elsa will be faced with the challenge of embracing vulnerability and navigating the complexities of her attachment style. She knows that if she wants to create a truly meaningful and fulfilling relationship with Alex, she must confront her fears and find the courage to step beyond the emotional fortress she had built around her heart. The battle within her will be tough, but Elsa is determined to break free from her past and find a path towards authentic emotional connection and love. Alex deserved it.

Chapter 4 | The Impact on Career

Elsa's attachment style not only affects her romantic relationships but also has a significant impact on her career journey. The fear of failure and rejection that stems from her fearful avoidant attachment style seeps into her professional life, influencing her choices and decisions.

Throughout her career, Elsa often finds herself hesitating to seek promotions or leadership positions. Despite her talent and qualifications, she holds back from taking on higher responsibilities, fearing that she might not live up to expectations or may face rejection if she tries and fails. This fear of failure becomes a self-fulfilling prophecy, as her reluctance to step out of her comfort zone prevents her from experiencing growth and advancement in her career.

Elsa's fear of rejection is deeply ingrained in her attachment style. She fears that if she puts herself forward for promotions or leadership roles, she might face criticism or negative feedback, which she interprets as a personal rejection. This fear becomes a significant barrier to her professional growth, holding her back from exploring new opportunities and challenging herself in her career.

In team settings, Elsa struggles with assertiveness and self-advocacy. She finds it difficult to assert her opinions and ideas, fearing that her contributions may be dismissed or criticized. This lack of confidence in her abilities prevents her from fully utilizing her potential and making a meaningful impact in her workplace.

Elsa's career journey also reflects her tendency to avoid seeking support or guidance from colleagues or mentors. She prefers to tackle challenges on her own, believing that relying on others emotionally might make her vulnerable to potential rejection or judgment. This self-reliance can hinder her ability to grow professionally, as she may miss out on valuable insights and opportunities for collaboration.

As Elsa refrains from taking risks and seeking advancement in her career, she becomes stuck in a cycle of stagnation. She watches her peers progress and achieve success while she remains in her comfort zone, feeling unfulfilled and undervalued.

Throughout her career journey, Elsa's attachment style manifests as a protective mechanism against potential failure and rejection. However, in the process, it also hinders her from reaching her full potential and finding true satisfaction in her professional life.

In the upcoming chapters of Elsa's story, she will have to confront her attachment-related fears in her career as well. With the help of self-awareness and a growing understanding of her attachment style's impact, Elsa will begin to explore ways to challenge her fears and embrace opportunities for growth and advancement.

As she navigates her career journey with a newfound sense of courage and self-acceptance, she will uncover her true potential and unlock new horizons of success and fulfillment in her professional life.

Chapter 5 | Recognizing Patterns

Elsa realizes that she has a tendency to gravitate towards partners who mirror her own attachment style or who have strong avoidant or anxious attachment tendencies. She unconsciously seeks out these familiar patterns, as they align with the emotional lands-cape she has become accustomed to since childhood.

In her past relationships, Elsa often found herself attracted to partners who seemed emotionally distant or aloof. She mistook their emotional unavailability as a sign of independence and strength, which initially drew her in. However, as the relationship progressed, she would become frustrated by their emotional detachment and yearn for deeper emotional connection.

On the other hand, she also encountered partners who displayed anxious attachment tendencies. These partners sought constant reassurance and closeness, which overwhelmed Elsa and triggered her fear of emotional suffocation. She felt torn between wanting to be there for her partner and feeling overwhelmed by their emotional demands.

Recognizing these patterns is both eye-opening and unsettling for Elsa. She comes to understand that her attachment style influences not only her own behaviors but also the dynamics that play out in her romantic relationships. The push-and-pull dynamics, emotional turbulence, and feelings of uncertainty are all a result of her fearful avoidant tendencies interacting with her partner's attachment style.

With this newfound awareness, Elsa begins to question the root of her attraction to partners who perpetuate these patterns. She understands that her attachment style is seeking a familiar emotional environment, even if it is not conducive to the deep emotional connection she truly desires.

As Elsa reflects on her past relationships, she realizes that her attachment style has been a powerful force, shaping the course of her romantic endeavors. Her therapist helps her to recognize, that while her attachment style is a part of who she is, it does not define her entirely.

With this understanding, she gains a sense of empowerment, knowing that with professional help, she has the power to break free from these repeating patterns and create healthier and more fulfilling relationships.

Elsa knows that transforming these patterns will require courage, consistency and vulnerability. And with the help of her therapist to hold her accountable and support her growth, she is determined to challenge her attachment-related fears and seek partners who are willing to embrace emotional intimacy with her. Elsa now understands that forming a meaningful connection will require taking risks and stepping into the discomfort of vulnerability.

In the upcoming chapters of her journey, Elsa will explore how to navigate her attachment style with intention and make conscious choices in her romantic relationships. With the help of her therapist, she will learn to seek partners who value emotional connection and are willing to work together towards building a secure and loving bond.

Chapter 6 | Unraveling Barriers

With continued therapy sessions, Elsa's self-awareness deepens, and she begins to realize that her fearful avoidant traits are hindering her from forming the deep connections she craves. She starts to explore ways to embrace vulnerability and confront her fears of emotional intimacy. This chapter depicts her struggle and growth as she takes steps towards creating a more secure attachment style.

With each introspective moment, Elsa begins to understand the patterns that have shaped her relationships and the root of her attachment-related fears. She recognizes that her fear of emotional intimacy, developed as a protective response to past experiences, has become a formidable barrier to the depth of connection she longs for.

Elsa has moments of vulnerability and clarity where she sees how her attachment style has played a role in her romantic endeavors. It finally dawns on her that her fear of rejection and abandonment have been at the forefront of her relationships, sabotaging her opportunities for authentic love and emotional fulfillment. This realization is both empowering and challenging for Elsa. On one hand, she feels a sense of relief in finally understanding the root of her attachment-related struggles. She acknowledges that her attachment style is a product of her past and not an inherent flaw in her character.

This newfound awareness helps her to cultivate self-compassion and acceptance, and recognizes that her fearful avoidant traits are simply a coping mechanism that she developed to survive emotionally turbulent times.

On the other hand, Elsa recognizes that this awareness calls for significant changes in her approach to relationships. She understands that in order to form the deep connections she craves; she must confront her fears and actively work towards embracing vulnerability. This is where her therapist was especially helpful. She was able to easily recognize and point out to Elsa, the patterns of behavior that she continued to use unconsciously, but wasn't aware of.

As her self-awareness deepens, Elsa learns to question her own actions and reactions in her relationships. With this newfound understanding, Elsa is motivated to break free from the shackles of her fearful avoidant traits. She knows that it won't be an easy journey, as the fears and habits she has developed over the years are deeply ingrained. However, she is committed to the process of growth and healing, knowing that the reward of authentic connection is worth the effort.

Through therapy, she learns new coping mechanisms to deal with her fear of emotional intimacy and develops communication skills to express her emotions and needs more openly.

As she continues to take small steps towards embracing vulnerability, Elsa starts to experience moments of emotional connection that she had previously thought were beyond her reach. Each instance of emotional openness becomes a stepping stone towards the deep connections she has always craved.

In the upcoming chapters of her journey, Elsa will encounter challenges and setbacks, but she remains committed to growth and healing. As she continues to unravel the barriers created by her fearful avoidant traits, she inches closer to forming the meaningful connections she craves. Elsa's self-awareness soon becomes a guiding light in her quest for emotional liberation and authentic love.

Chapter 7 | The Impact on Partners

Elsa's romantic partners find themselves navigating a complex emotional landscape, influenced by her fearful avoidant tendencies. As they embark on relationships with her, they encounter both the allure of her charm and the challenges posed by her attachment style.

For some partners, Elsa's emotional fluctuations and fear of commitment can be overwhelming. At the beginning of the relationship, they are drawn to her independence and her ability to keep things light and carefree. However, as the relationship deepens, they usually start to sense Elsa's emotional walls and her reluctance to fully open up. Her hesitancy to commit can lead to uncertainty and frustration for her partner, as they may not fully understand the reasons behind her emotional distance.

As the relationship progresses, Elsa's partners may feel like they are walking on eggshells, unsure of how to navigate her moments of emotional withdrawal and her seemingly conflicting desires for closeness and distance. They may struggle to decode her emotional signals and find it challenging to get a clear sense of where they stand in the relationship. Some partners may even attempt to confront Elsa about her emotional fluctuations and fear of commitment, seeking reassurance and clarity.

However, these conversations can be emotionally charged, as Elsa grapples with her own internal conflicts. Her partners may find it challenging to break through her emotional barriers, leaving them feeling disconnected and unfulfilled in the relationship.

On the other hand, some partners may be naturally drawn to Elsa's emotional independence, as they may also have avoidant tendencies. They may appreciate the space she provides and the ease with which she navigates her own emotions. However, as the relationship progresses, they may find themselves craving deeper emotional intimacy and a stronger sense of connection, which can be difficult to achieve with Elsa's fearful avoidant attachment style.

For partners who seek emotional closeness and connection, Elsa's fear of vulnerability can be a source of frustration and disappointment. They may feel that she holds back emotionally, making it challenging for the relationship to progress beyond a certain level of intimacy. They may yearn for more emotional reciprocity and depth, but find it elusive in the face of Elsa's attachment-related fears.

As Elsa's romantic partners continue to navigate her fearful avoidant tendencies, they may wrestle with their own emotions and desires. Some may choose to stay in the relationship, drawn to her charm and hoping for a breakthrough in emotional intimacy. Others may reach a point where they realize that their needs for emotional connection are not being met, leading them to reevaluate the relationship.

Each partner's experience is unique, influenced by their own attachment styles and desires for emotional connection. As Elsa continues her journey of self-awareness and growth, she will have to confront these patterns in her relationships and find a path towards building more secure and fulfilling connections with her partners.

Chapter 8 | Breaking Free from Old Patterns

In this chapter, Elsa begins to challenge her old patterns and defenses. She learns to communicate her feelings and needs more openly and takes proactive steps to address her fears. We witness her making efforts to create a secure emotional bond with her romantic partner, breaking free from the cycle of emotional distance.

She starts to share her emotions with Alex, expressing her fears, desires, and uncertainties. At times, her forward movement is sabotaged by familiar feeling of the fear of being rejected and although this newfound openness is both liberating and terrifying, Elsa sometimes becomes overwhelmed with the fear that her partners might judge or reject her for her true feelings.

She addresses these concerns with her therapist, and engages in open and honest conversations about her fear of commitment. Her therapist encourages her to share her journey of self-discovery and growth with her partner, allowing them to understand the complexities of her emotional landscape. She explains, that through these conversations, Elsa will help her partner comprehend the reasons behind her emotional fluctuations and fear of commitment, fostering a deeper level of understanding and empathy in the relationship.

She is given self-soothing techniques which she can use when she feels overwhelmed by emotional intimacy, learning to comfort herself and find stability within her own emotions. This newfound self-compassion allows her to navigate moments of vulnerability with greater ease.

As she challenges her old patterns and defenses, Elsa learns to create healthier boundaries in her relationships. She recognizes the importance of balancing emotional closeness with personal space and independence for both herself and her partner. This allows her to maintain a sense of self while also nurturing the emotional connection with Alex.

Through therapy and self-reflection, Elsa explores techniques to cope with her fear of rejection and abandonment. She recognizes that these fears are deeply ingrained but not insurmountable. Elsa learns how to challenge the automatic thoughts and beliefs that arise in moments of emotional distress, replacing them with more constructive and positive thoughts.

With time and practice, Elsa notices the positive impact of her efforts. She feels more in control of her emotions and less overwhelmed by her attachment-related fears. As she continues to challenge her old patterns and defenses, she realizes that vulnerability is not a sign of weakness, but rather a gateway to authenticity and emotional connection.

As her healing process progresses, Elsa finds that as she communicates her feelings and needs more openly, and Alex responds with understanding and compassion. He appreciates her efforts to break free from her old patterns and supports her in her journey of growth.

Chapter 9 | Embracing Change Through Emotional Intimacy

As Elsa continues her journey of growth, we witness the positive changes in her romantic relationships and personal life. She learns to appreciate emotional intimacy and understands that vulnerability can lead to deeper connections. This chapter showcases her willingness to embrace change and the rewards it brings to her relationships and overall well-being.

Soon her partner recognizes a profound transformation in her perception of emotional intimacy. Through continued efforts to challenge her fearful avoidant attachment style and embrace vulnerability, Elsa learns to appreciate the depth and richness of emotional connection. With each step towards vulnerability, Elsa learns that allowing herself to be emotionally open and authentic with her partners fosters a sense of trust and closeness that she had never experienced before.

Her willingness to share her emotions and vulnerabilities with her partners creates a safe and nurturing space for them to reciprocate. As she communicates her feelings and needs more openly, her partners respond with compassion and empathy.

This mutual exchange of emotional openness forms the foundation for deeper and more meaningful connections. She learns that vulnerability and openness enable her to express her desires, fears, and dreams, fostering a sense of emotional connection that goes beyond surface-level interactions.

Her newfound appreciation for emotional intimacy also extends to other areas of her life. In her friendships and family relationships, she starts to cultivate deeper connections by allowing herself to be vulnerable and express her emotions honestly.

As she navigates the complexities of emotional intimacy, Elsa also learns to embrace the ebb and flow of emotions in her relationships. She understands that emotional closeness does not mean a constant state of perfect harmony, but rather an acceptance of the highs and lows that come with genuine connection.

Elsa begins to view vulnerability as a pathway to growth and healing. She recognizes that embracing vulnerability is a courageous act that allows her to break free from her old patterns and foster more authentic and fulfilling relationships.

As the chapter unfolds, Elsa reflects on her transformation and the path that led her to embrace emotional intimacy. She knows that the journey is ongoing and that vulnerability will always be a part of her growth process. But she also understands that the rewards of genuine emotional connection are immeasurable and worth every step along the way.

Elsa now looks forward to a future filled with deep connections and authentic love. She knows that by embracing emotional intimacy, she has opened herself up to a world of possibilities and experiences that she once believed were beyond her reach. Elsa's journey of growth and transformation serves as an inspiring testament to the power of vulnerability and the beauty of emotional intimacy in shaping meaningful and fulfilling relationships.

Chapter 10 | Finding Hope and Acceptance

In this final chapter, Elsa comes to a place of hope and acceptance. She recognizes that her fearful avoidant attachment style is a part of who she is, but it doesn't define her entirely. Through perseverance, consistency, and therapy, Elsa has learned to navigate her attachment challenges and create healthier relationships.

We see her embracing hope for the future, knowing that she now has the tools to form meaningful connections and find fulfillment in both her career and personal life. With each step she takes towards vulnerability and emotional intimacy, Elsa has learned to embrace her authentic self.

She acknowledges that her fearful avoidant tendencies are a natural response to her past experiences and are deeply ingrained in her being. However, she no longer views them as flaws or limitations and now values the lessons she learned from her past relationship failures.

Elsa recognizes that her attachment style has influenced her choices and behaviors in relationships, but it doesn't mean she is destined to repeat the patterns of her past. Instead, she now understands that she has the power to challenge these patterns and create new narratives in her life.

Elsa has cultivated a sense of hope for her future relationships. She knows that by being aware of her attachment style and its impact, she can make more conscious choices in her romantic partnerships. She understands that she deserves love and emotional fulfillment and is willing to work towards creating the connections she craves.

The acceptance of her attachment style brings Elsa a sense of peace and self-compassion. She realizes that she is not alone in her struggles, as many people grapple with their attachment patterns. With this newfound acceptance, Elsa releases the weight of self-judgment and replaces it with understanding and kindness towards herself.

As Elsa reflects on her journey, she also acknowledges the growth and transformation she has experienced. She celebrates the moments of vulnerability and emotional intimacy she embraced along the way, recognizing that each step was a testament to her strength and courage.

In the concluding moments of her journey, Elsa understands that her attachment style is just one aspect of her multifaceted personality. She knows that she is more than her fears and past experiences. She is a complex and evolving individual with the capacity for love, compassion, and growth.

She now looks forward to her future with a sense of hope and excitement and knows that her journey of growth and acceptance will continue. She is now eager and more capable to face whatever comes her way. With her newfound understanding of herself and her attachment style, she is better equipped to navigate the complexities of relationships and embrace emotional intimacy.

In the end, Elsa's story serves as a powerful reminder that self-awareness and acceptance can lead to transformative change. Her journey of hope and acceptance inspires others to confront their own attachment-related struggles and is a testament to the resilience of the human spirit, and the capacity for growth and healing, even in the face of past challenges.

CASSIE | THE ANXIOUS PREOCCUPIED ATTACHMENT

Chapter 1 | The Roots of Anxious Attachment

Cassie, like most young women, yearns for the love and connection a relationship can bring. As we delve into her world, we encounter a tapestry of emotions intricately woven by her anxious preoccupied attachment style, and discovers how it affects her relationships.

A striking blend of ambition, creative brilliance and vulnerability, Cassie has the potential to excel in her career as a marketing executive. But behind her poised exterior lies a heart in constant turmoil; tangled in an intricate web of anxious thoughts and emotions, which has crippled her potential of rising in her career.

From an early age, Cassie struggles with a deep-seated fear of rejection and fear of abandonment. Growing up in a home where love, stands as both a beacon of joy and a labyrinth of inconsistencies, she learned to seek constant reassurance to validate her worth. The echoes of her childhood experiences helped shape her attachment style, leaving her to experience much anxiety in her relationships.

Growing up in a household where nurturing was inconsistent, Cassie learned to navigate her feelings and emotions with a sense of uncertainty. Her parent's well-intentioned yet emotionally inconsistent care, inadvertently planted the seeds of her attachment style.

Affection and praise were often withheld, leaving Cassie longing for validation and yearning for a love that felt secure and unwavering. As a child, Cassie tried to earn her parents' love and approval through achievements, people pleasing, and perfect behavior.

The notion that love was contingent upon her performance instilled in her a deep fear of rejection, and she constantly sought reassurance that she was worthy of being loved. Unfortunately, that reassurance was fleeting, leaving her anxious and yearning for more.

In her romantic relationships, anxiety becomes even more pronounced because of the level of emotional connection required. Cassie's attachment style manifests as an overwhelming need for emotional closeness with her romantic partners. The fear of being unloved and abandoned pushes her to seek constant affirmation and validation, often becoming engulfed in worry over the slightest change in her partner's behavior.

Her mind becomes a labyrinth of insecurities, causing her to overanalyze every interaction and second-guess her partner's intentions. When she enters a new relationship, her heart is flooded with hope and excitement. However, as the connection deepens, so does her anxiety. She becomes preoccupied with thoughts of potential rejection, leading her to seek constant validation and reassurance from her partner. She longs for constant contact and feels intense emotions when apart, often fearing that her partner may forget about her or lose interest.

In the early stages of dating, Cassie may come across as overbearing or too eager, as she seeks to establish a strong emotional bond quickly. Her anxious preoccupied traits often cause her to neglect her own needs and desires, prioritizing her partner's wishes above her own in the quest for acceptance and love.

As Cassie's romantic relationships progresses, she loses herself and morphs into the identity of her partner, but doesn't realize that her fear of abandonment from others, also extends in her abandoning herself. Her partner becomes her whole world, and she disengages from her friends and family members, to spend all her time with her new partner.

With her love interests, she may become excessively sensitive to perceived signs of emotional distance. Any slight change in her partner's behavior may trigger intense worry and fear of rejection, leading her to bombard them with messages or behave in ways she believes will force their attention, in an attempt to protect herself from potential hurt.

For Cassie, any attention is still attention. As a result, she may behave in ways to make her partner jealous, believing that this behavior will draw them back to her. However, this is a dangerous game to play, since this type of behavior usually serves to build mistrust in her partners.

Memories of early negative experiences of her early relationships are frequent visitors in Cassie's mind. They linger like faint whispers, solidifying the foundation of her anxious preoccupied attachment style.

As we delve into her past, we uncover the echoes of her childhood experiences, that have left a profound impact on her heart and the way she views love and connection.

The unpredictable nature of her parents' emotional availability instilled a deep fear of abandonment in Cassie. She never knew when she would receive love and affection, leaving her in a perpetual state of anxiety and uncertainty.

As a child, she internalized the belief that love was scarce and conditional, and that she had to constantly prove her worth to receive it. The lack of emotional attunement in her early relationships left Cassie feeling unseen and unheard. In the absence of consistent emotional support, she developed a belief that she was not enough, and that she had to earn love through constant effort.

As Cassie grew older, her anxious preoccupied attachment style began to emerge in her friendships and romantic relationships. She found herself becoming overly dependent on others for validation and emotional support, fearing that any sign of emotional distance could lead to abandonment.

In her teenage years, Cassie experienced her first romantic relationship, which further solidified her attachment style. The fear of losing her partner consumed her, leading her to become clingy and possessive. She craved constant reassurance that she was loved, which put a strain on the relationship and eventually led to its end.

Throughout her formative years, Cassie's attachment style was reinforced by a series of short-lived friendships and relationships. Each experience served as a mirror, reflecting her deepest fears and insecurities back at her. Despite her efforts to find lasting love and connection, she seemed trapped in a cycle of heartbreak and longing.

Cassie yearns to break free from the grip of her anxious preoccupied attachment style. She knows that her path to healing lies in understanding the roots of her fears and embracing the truths of her past. But untangling the web of emotions and unlearning deeply ingrained patterns proves to be no easy feat.

In her romantic relationships, she often sought out partners who mirrored the emotional unavailability and inconsistency of her parents, unknowingly repeating patterns from her past.

As her relationships deepens, Cassie became increasingly sensitive to any perceived signs of emotional distance or rejection. Her anxieties would escalate, leading her to overanalyze and cling to her partner in a desperate attempt to maintain closeness and security.

Her childhood dynamics also influenced her communication style, as she struggled to express her needs and emotions openly. The fear of being rejected or dismissed led her to suppress her true feelings, further exacerbating the emotional distance in her relationships.

The lack of consistent emotional attunement in her early years also affected Cassie's ability to trust others and herself. The absence of a secure emotional anchor made her vulnerable to seeking validation from external sources, leading to a perpetual cycle of seeking reassurance and feeling unfulfilled.

As Cassie explores her childhood dynamics and their impact on her present-day challenges, she begins to recognize the roots of her attachment style. She acknowledges that her anxieties and fears are not inherent flaws, but rather a reflection of her past experiences.

Chapter 2 | Love's First Whirlwind

Cassie soon encounters Jake, and a whirlwind of emotions ensue. Amidst the cacophony of life, Cassie's heart finds its way to a heartfelt connection in her first adult relationship. Their encounter sparks a whirlwind of emotions, unveiling the intricacies of Cassie's anxious preoccupied attachment style as she navigates the uncharted territory of love.

As Cassie and Jake's paths intertwine, a flutter of excitement courses through her veins. She is drawn to Jake's charm and warmth, finding solace in his attentive presence. Their shared laughter and easy conversations create a sense of comfort she had never experienced before.

Yet, amidst the blossoming romance, a wave of anxiety engulfs Cassie. Her heart is caught in the currents of uncertainty, fearing that the love she has found might slip through her fingers. Her mind becomes a labyrinth of questions and doubts, leaving her burdened under the weight of her anxieties.

As their relationship progresses, Cassie's attachment challenges become evident as she seeks constant reassurance from Jake. She yearns for him to verbalize his affection and commitment, yearning for the certainty that their love is steadfast and secure. The fear of being abandoned lingers like a shadow, causing her to clutch tightly onto him, desperately seeking validation and confirmation that their love is secure.

As their bond deepens, so does the intensity of Cassie's emotions. She is enamored by Jake's affectionate gestures, cherishing each moment they spend together. But as the days pass, she finds herself entangled in a web of worry. Her anxious thoughts weave scenarios of potential rejection, causing her to feel on edge and vulnerable. "Why can't I just enjoy what we have now?" she keeps asking herself. But the answer doesn't come. Instead, the fear of being abandoned persists and screams in every quiet moment.

Jake, unfamiliar with the complexities of attachment styles, attempts to provide reassurance. Yet, despite his efforts, Cassie's need for validation persists. She worries that any change in Jake's behavior might signal a loss of interest, and her mind becomes consumed by overthinking and overanalyzing every interaction and micro-expressions.

As their love deepens, so does Cassie's fear of losing it. She oscillates between moments of euphoria and those of anxious uncertainty, leaving her emotionally exhausted. The intensity of her emotions becomes overwhelming, and she begins to question whether love is meant to be this tumultuous. She yearns to be authentic with Jake, to share her struggles, yet the fear of losing him or pushing him away holds her back.

In the midst of this whirlwind, Cassie grapples with the realization that her outbursts of emotions and clingy behavior, has the power to shape her love and relationships. She becomes aware of how her anxieties might create barriers between her and Jake, preventing her from fully embracing the love she desires.

As Cassie continues her journey through love's intricate terrain, she learns that there is something called "attachment styles" that seem to explain her behavior in relationships. She discovers that the anxious preoccupied attachment style, describes many of the traits she has and her anxious approach to relationships.

Cassie longs to find solace in the warmth of her partner's love, as she seeks the affection and attention a relationship can offer. She longs for a sense of security that she cherishes deeply. Yet, Cassie is aware that even in the arms of love, the tendrils of her anxious preoccupied traits find their way into her heart, tightening their grip on her emotions. Like a delicate dance between desire and fear, her traits shape the dynamics of her relationship, leaving her torn between the yearning for closeness and the fear of rejection.

As her relationship with Jake deepens, so does Cassie's need for reassurance. She craves constant affirmations of his love; desperate for words that will quiet the storm of anxieties within her, and so she clings to his affectionate gestures, seeking confirmation that she is valued, wanted and cherished.

With each interaction, her mind becomes a minefield of questions and uncertainties. Is he still interested? Does he truly love me? These doubts dance in her thoughts, leaving her feeling vulnerable and exposed. And it seems that even though Jake gave her no reason to doubt his love, she just couldn't trust that his love for her would last.

Cassie's anxious preoccupied traits also influences her communication style. She often finds herself overthinking everything Jake does, while at the same time, feels afraid that expressing her emotions openly might drive him away. As a result, she stuffs her feelings, tucking her anxieties beneath a smile, and hoping he will perceive her emotional struggles by somehow reading her mind.

The smallest changes in Jake's behavior become magnified, igniting a cascade of worries. Her attachment style leads her to interpret any perceived distance as a sign of impending rejection, and she panics at the thought of losing him.

In moments of emotional distance, however subtle, the ache of abandonment reverberates through Cassie's being. Each unanswered text or missed call sends her thoughts spiraling into a vortex of doubt. The fear that Jake might withdraw his affection, trigger an instinctual response to seek reassurance.

In her efforts to maintain closeness, Cassie becomes overly accommodating, putting her partner's needs above her own. She may suppress her desires, fearing that expressing them might cause conflict or drive him away. As a result, she prioritizes his emotional needs over her own, at times neglecting her own well-being in the process; further sliding down the rabbit hole of despair.

Her mind becomes a battleground of conflicting thoughts. She yearns for constant validation, seeking the reassurance that she is cherished and valued.

Yet, with each plea for affection, she fears pushing him away, terrified that her insecurities will become a burden to him. She grapples with the knowledge that her behavior may create a self-fulfilling prophecy, driving her partner away in her pursuit of constant reassurance.

Although Cassie recognizes the need to confront her anxieties and communicate her needs more openly, she feels crippled to do anything about it. She finally realizes that she needed help from someone who understands what might be happening to her and found a therapist specializing in attachment styles.

With the help of her therapist, she begins the journey of managing her unconscious patterns of behavior and replacing them with healthier behaviors on the way to becoming more secure. Cassie begins to acknowledge the need to find balance and learns that seeking reassurance is natural, but that she must also nurture her own emotional well-being. As she embarks on a journey of self-discovery, she is guided by her therapist to find a sense of security within herself rather than relying solely on external validation. With a commitment to growth and change, she takes the first steps towards forming more secure connections and finding the love and emotional fulfillment she deserves.

Cassie finds the courage to face her past and its lingering effects on her present. As she embarks on a journey of self-discovery and healing, she knows that untangling the echoes of her past is the key to forging more secure and fulfilling connections in her future.

She is encouraged to take small steps towards sharing her anxieties with Jake, unveiling the layers of her heart that have been guarded for so long. Each day, Cassie finds the courage to face her past and its lingering effects on her present.

Chapter 3 | Need for Emotional Assurance

As their love story unfolds, Jake becomes more attuned to the intricacies of Cassie's attachment style. He learns to navigate the delicate balance between providing support and giving her the reassurance that he's in their relationship for the long haul. He understands that her anxious preoccupied traits are not a reflection of her love for him, but rather a reflection of her past experiences.

When Cassie's finds herself slipping back into her former patterns of anxiety and fears of abandonment, she learns to be open with Jake about how she feels. She now understands that Jake is not her enemy and that a simple conversation can allow Jake to reassure her that her fears are unfounded.

As their love story deepens, Jake remains a steadfast anchor for Cassie. His patience and understanding provides a sense of security that she treasures deeply. Yet, she knows that true growth lies in finding a sense of security within herself, untangling the threads of her anxieties and finding her own emotional balance.

There are times that Cassie's constant need for reassurance places an emotional burden on their relationship, but Jake remains steadfast in his support for Cassie. As she sees Jake's consistency in his love and care for her, despite the burden she places on him, she soon becomes more assured that Jake can be trusted to stay. Soon, her constant need for reassurance becomes less and less and her bouts of jealousy, fear of abandonment and possesiveness is vastly reduced.

With self-awareness as her guide, Cassie embarks on a journey of healing. She seeks to understand the roots of her attachment style and develop coping mechanisms to manage her anxieties. She learns to communicate her needs openly and honestly, embracing vulnerability as a source of strength rather than a source of fear.

Her therapist points out to Cassie, that one of the greatest challenges she faces is distinguishing between genuine concerns and irrational anxieties. Her attachment style often leads her to interpret harmless situations as potential threats to her relationship. Learning to differentiate between legitimate concerns and unfounded fears becomes a pivotal step in managing her anxious thoughts.

While Jake is understanding and patient, her need for validation can create moments of tension. Learning to strike a balance between leaning on her partner for support and developing inner emotional security is an ongoing process for them both.

As she ventures on the path of self-discovery and healing, Cassie also learns the importance of self-compassion. She acknowledges that her anxious preoccupied attachment style is not a flaw but a natural response to her life experiences. Embracing self-compassion allows her to treat herself with gentleness and understanding as she navigates the challenges that arise.

Chapter 4 | The Balancing Act

Cassie's attachment style also seeps into the fabric of her career journey, influencing the way she navigates the professional landscape. The interplay between her anxious preoccupied traits and her pursuit of success creates a delicate dance of challenges and triumphs in the realm of work.

In her career, Cassie's attachment style manifests in various ways. The fear of rejection and abandonment that permeates her personal relationships finds echoes in her professional life. She yearns for approval and validation from her superiors and colleagues, seeking constant reassurance that her work is valued and appreciated.

The constant need for reassurance also seeps into her decision-making process. Cassie may find herself hesitant to take risks or pursue opportunities that she perceives as potentially leading to rejection or failure. This fear of putting herself out there can hinder her from fully embracing her professional growth and taking on new challenges.

Similarly, her anxious preoccupied attachment style may lead her to become overly accommodating in her interactions with others. She may be hesitant to assert herself or express her opinions out of fear that doing so could lead to conflict or rejection. As a result, she may struggle to advocate for her ideas or negotiate for her own needs, potentially hindering her career progression.

In moments of stress or pressure, Cassie's attachment style may intensify, causing her to experience emotional flooding in her professional life as well. The overwhelming surge of anxious thoughts and emotions can impact her ability to focus and make clear decisions, potentially affecting her performance at work.

Additionally, Cassie's attachment style may also influence her approach to relationships with colleagues and superiors. She may develop anxious attachments to mentors or role models, seeking validation and guidance from them in a way that mirrors her personal relationships.

However, despite the challenges her attachment style presents, Cassie's career journey is not devoid of triumphs. Her strong sense of empathy and emotional intelligence can be valuable assets in her professional interactions, allowing her to understand and connect with others on a deeper level.

As she continues to explore her attachment style through therapy and self-reflection, Cassie gains insights into how her anxious preoccupied traits influence her career decisions and interactions. She begins to challenge her old patterns and develop strategies to manage her anxieties in the professional sphere.

With time and effort, Cassie learns to strike a balance between seeking validation and finding inner fulfillment in her career. She recognizes that her worth is not solely defined by external recognition, but by the impact she makes and the growth she experiences.

Recognizing that failure is a natural part of growth, Cassie learns to view setbacks as opportunities for learning and development rather than moments of defeat. She discovers that embracing vulnerability and taking calculated risks can lead to personal and professional growth, opening doors to new possibilities.

In her pursuit of personal and professional fulfillment, Cassie finds strength in embracing the discomfort of uncertainty. She realizes that the fear of criticism can be a catalyst for improvement and that seeking validation from within herself is just as crucial as seeking it from others.

Embracing self-compassion and authenticity, Cassie navigates the intersections of love and work, seeking to forge a path that integrates her attachment style into a source of strength rather than a limitation. As she continues to grow both personally and professionally, she finds empowerment in embracing her whole self, knowing that her attachment style is a part of her, but it doesn't define the entirety of her journey.

Chapter 5 | Seeking Solace in Relationships

Cassie's attachment style has a profound impact not only on her own emotions but also on her partner's sense of responsibility and emotional burden within their relationship.

Her constant need for reassurance and validation places a significant emotional burden on Jake. The fear of rejection and abandonment that characterizes her attachment style leaves her seeking constant comfort and validation, often turning to her partner to fill the void of her insecurities.

As her partner, they may feel a sense of responsibility to provide the emotional support and reassurance that Cassie needs. While they may want to be there for her and offer comfort, the weight of this emotional burden can be overwhelming, especially if they have their struggles and stressors to manage as well.

For someone with this attachment style, a securely attached individual will be the best chance for success, as they will have the emotional bandwidth to handle the stress this relationship can bring.

Cassie's attachment style may create a dynamic where her partner feels responsible for managing her emotions and self-esteem. This dynamic can lead to feelings of frustration or exhaustion, as they try to meet her constant need for validation and reassurance while also managing their own emotional well-being.

In moments of emotional distance or conflict, Cassie's attachment style may amplify her partner's feelings of inadequacy or frustration. Despite their efforts to support her, they may struggle to provide the level of reassurance she seeks, leading to misunderstandings and emotional tension.

Her partner's sense of responsibility in managing her emotional well-being may lead them to suppress their own feelings and needs. They may prioritize her emotional needs above their own, leading to a lack of balance in the relationship and potential long-term strain.

Furthermore, Cassie's attachment style can also influence how her partner communicates their own emotions and concerns. They may hesitate to express their frustrations or share their struggles, fearing that it may add to her emotional burden or trigger her anxieties.

By seeking out therapy from a professional, Cassie also explores ways to build her own emotional resilience and coping mechanisms. By relying on a support network beyond her romantic relationship, she takes proactive steps to reduce her partner's emotional burden and cultivate self-reliance and find equilibrium that allows for both vulnerability and self-sufficiency, recognizing that emotional burdens should be shared and not solely carried by one partner.

Chapter 6 | Unraveling Emotional Dependence and Boundaries

Cassie's attachment style fosters emotional dependence within her romantic relationships. In moments of emotional distress, Cassie may become overly reliant on her partner to soothe her anxieties and provide a sense of security. This emotional dependence can lead to her partner feeling overwhelmed by the responsibility of being her sole source of comfort and stability.

As the emotional dynamics in her relationships unfold, Cassie grapples with the struggle to create healthy boundaries. Her attachment style prompts her to blur the lines between her own emotions and those of her partner, making it challenging to distinguish where one person's feelings end and the other's begin.

This lack of boundaries can lead to emotional enmeshment, where Cassie and her partner become emotionally entangled to the point where it becomes difficult to maintain a sense of individuality and autonomy. The lack of space for personal growth and self-expression may lead to tension and a sense of suffocation.

Moreover, Cassie's emotional dependence may also manifest in clingy behavior or an inability to spend time apart from her partner. The fear of losing them or being left alone intensifies her desire for closeness, at times causing her to overlook the importance of personal space and independence.

With the help of her therapist, she becomes more aware of these patterns, and Cassie begins to reflect on the impact of emotional dependence on her relationships. She acknowledges that true intimacy requires a balance of closeness and individuality, understanding that healthy boundaries are essential for a sustainable and thriving connection.

In therapy and through self-reflection, Cassie explores ways to cultivate emotional autonomy and establish healthy boundaries within her relationships. She learns to regulate her emotions and manage her anxieties independently, while still acknowledging the importance of seeking support from her partner when needed.

Her partner's support and understanding play a crucial role in this journey. They encourage open communication and the expression of individual needs and emotions, creating a safe space for both Cassie and themselves to be emotionally independent and interdependent.

As she becomes more aware of these patterns, Cassie strives to break free from the maze of over-analysis and catastrophizing. Through therapy and self-reflection, she learns to recognize when her anxious thoughts are spiraling and is armed with strategies from her therapist to interrupt the cycle.

Cassie finds solace in grounding techniques, such as mindfulness and deep breathing, to bring herself back to the present moment and curb the tendency to overanalyze. She also practices challenging her catastrophizing thoughts, considering alternative perspectives and reframing her fears.

In her communication with Jake, Cassie becomes more transparent about her struggles with over-analysis and catastrophizing. By sharing her vulnerability and seeking his understanding, they create a space for open dialogue and support in navigating these challenges together.

Chapter 7 | Strengthening Communication

As we delve into this chapter, we explore how her attachment style impacts her capacity to express herself honestly and authentically within her relationship.

Communication, a cornerstone of any healthy relationship, becomes a labyrinth of challenges for Cassie. Her fear of rejection and the need for constant reassurance hinder her from openly sharing her thoughts, feelings, and needs with her partner. The worry of being misunderstood or perceived as needy keeps her emotions tightly guarded, locked behind the walls of her anxious heart.

In moments of vulnerability, Cassie may find herself hesitating to express her true emotions. The fear of overwhelming or burdening Jake with her feelings causes her to withdraw, leaving important aspects of herself unspoken and unexplored. At other time, she expects Jake to somehow read her thoughts and come up with a solution.

Her attachment style also influences the tone and tenor of her communication. The constant need for reassurance may lead her to seek validation in her interactions with Jake, prompting her to fish for compliments or affirmation. Her over-analysis of every conversation may cause her to read too much into his words, leading to misunderstandings and emotional tension.

Moreover, her anxious preoccupied attachment style may also prompt her to withhold her emotions to avoid conflict or rejection. The fear of vulnerability and emotional exposure keeps her from communicating her genuine needs, creating a disconnect between her internal experiences and her outward expression.

Through therapy and self-reflection, she begins to recognize how her attachment style impacts her ability to communicate openly and authentically. Cassie takes proactive steps to break free from the shackles of fearful expression. She starts to challenge her fears of vulnerability, learning to trust in the authenticity of her emotions and the strength of her connection with Jake.

Chapter 8 | A Journey Towards Secure Connections

Therapy becomes a journey of self-compassion and understanding for Cassie. She begins to see her anxious preoccupied attachment style not as a flaw but as a natural response to past emotional wounds. This shift in perspective allows her to embrace her vulnerabilities with greater acceptance and kindness.

As she gains self-awareness, Cassie starts to recognize the impact of her attachment style on her relationships, particularly with Jake. Through open discussions with her therapist, she begins to understand how her fears and insecurities influence her perceptions and interactions.

Her therapist guides her in developing coping mechanisms for managing her anxious thoughts and emotions. Together, they work on strategies to interrupt the cycle of over-analysis and catastrophizing, fostering a more balanced perspective in her relationships.

Beyond therapy, Cassie also seeks self-help resources such as books, articles, and workshops on attachment theory. These resources provide her with additional insights and practical tools to navigate the challenges of her attachment style.

As she continues her journey of self-awareness and growth, Cassie engages in practices that promote emotional resilience and well-being. Mindfulness and meditation become daily rituals that help her ground herself in the present moment, reducing the grip of anxious thoughts.

The self-help resources also empower her to foster emotional autonomy and establish healthy boundaries within her relationships. She learns to communicate her needs and feelings more openly, creating a space for authentic expression and emotional exchange with Jake.

Throughout her journey, Cassie's relationship with Jake evolves as well. Their conversations become more honest and vulnerable, and they support each other in their respective journeys of self-discovery and growth.

Guided by her therapist, Cassie takes intentional steps towards finding a more secure and balanced approach to love and connection. Through their collaborative efforts, she discovers the transformative power of self-awareness and personal growth in reshaping her attachment style and fostering a healthier relationship with herself and others. Some of the tools she learned were:

- Identifying Triggers: Cassie begins by identifying her triggers, situations, or interactions that intensify her anxious preoccupied attachment style. By recognizing these triggers, she gains greater awareness of the patterns that influence her emotions and behaviors.
- Challenging Anxious Thoughts: With her therapist's guidance, Cassie learns to challenge her anxious thoughts and negative self-perceptions. She reframes her fears of rejection and abandonment, replacing them with more balanced and realistic perspectives.
- Mindfulness and Grounding: Cassie incorporates mindfulness and grounding techniques into her daily routine. These practices help her stay present in the moment and reduce the grip of anxious thoughts, fostering emotional resilience and a sense of inner calm.

- Building Emotional Autonomy: Cassie works on cultivating emotional autonomy by developing a stronger sense of self-worth and self-compassion. She learns that her worthiness is not dependent on external validation, but rather an inherent aspect of who she is.
- Establishing Healthy Boundaries: Guided by her therapist, Cassie sets clear and healthy boundaries in her relationships. She learns to communicate her needs and preferences while also respecting the boundaries of others, creating a balanced exchange of emotions and support.
- Embracing Vulnerability: Through therapy, Cassie gains a deeper understanding of the beauty and power of vulnerability. She learns that vulnerability is not a weakness but a courageous act of authenticity that fosters emotional intimacy and connection.
- Emphasizing Self-Care: Cassie prioritizes self-care and self-compassion in her life. She recognizes the importance of nurturing her emotional well-being and taking time for activities that bring her joy and fulfillment.
- Embracing Imperfection: As she continues to grow, Cassie learns to embrace imperfection in herself and her relationships.
- She recognizes that all relationships have ups and downs, and it's okay to make mistakes along the way.
- Open Communication: Cassie and her therapist work on improving her communication skills, encouraging her to express her feelings and needs more openly in her relationship with Jake. This newfound openness enhances emotional connection and mutual understanding.

- Celebrating Progress: Throughout her journey, Cassie celebrates her progress, both big and small. She acknowledges the steps she has taken towards a more secure attachment style and embraces the growth that comes with each new challenge.

As Cassie implements these steps and embraces a more secure and balanced approach to love and connection, her relationship with Jake flourishes. They build a foundation of trust, understanding, and emotional support, fostering a relationship that allows for both intimacy and individuality.

Chapter 9 | Unraveling of Threads

As Cassie's journey of self-awareness and growth unfolds, she begins to observe her newfound ability to navigate emotional intimacy and communicate her needs with greater ease and authenticity. With guidance from her therapist, Cassie learns to question the voices in her head that tells her she is unworthy of love and overwhelms her with feelings of fear of being abandoned and unloved.

As Cassie's journey of self-awareness and growth continues, she envisions a future filled with possibilities for secure connections and fulfillment in both love and career. The transformation she has undergone has laid the groundwork for a life rich with emotional authenticity, personal growth, and the ability to trust that those around her will not always abandon her.

In her relationship with Jake, Cassie experiences the beauty of a secure attachment. Their emotional connection is nurtured by open communication, mutual understanding, and a willingness to be patient with each other. They celebrate each other's successes and support one another during challenges, fostering a sense of emotional safety and trust that deepens with time.

Cassie's newfound ability to trust that not everyone is going to abandon her, also extends to her friendships and family relationships. She cherishes her support network and actively fosters connections with others based on authenticity and emotional reciprocity.

As she continues to invest in self-awareness of her unconscious response to life situations, Cassie finds fulfillment in her career as well. Her newfound confidence allows her to pursue opportunities that once felt intimidating. She takes risks, unafraid of the possibility of failure, knowing that her worth is not tied to external achievements. Cassie begins to embrace challenges and seeks out avenues for growth. She acknowledges her strengths and seeks support when needed, creating a fulfilling and supportive work environment.

The journey of self-awareness and growth has also led Cassie to embrace a greater sense of self-compassion and acceptance. She recognizes that she is a work in progress and that personal growth is an ongoing journey. Instead of criticizing herself for imperfections, she celebrates her efforts to grow and evolve, nurturing a kinder and more loving relationship with herself.

In her future, Cassie envisions a life enriched by secure connections, meaningful relationships, and a career that aligns with her passions and values. She continues to challenge her fear of the unknown and habits of overthinking, and is now more open to learning and evolving in her relationships and career.

Her therapist continues to encourage her to remain anchored in the present moment, embracing the beauty of love and connection that comes with emotional authenticity and trust. She appreciates the joy and fulfillment that secure connections bring, savoring each moment as it unfolds.

In her journey towards healing, Cassie moves closer to a life that is rich with love, connection, and fulfillment in both her personal and professional spheres. In the end, Cassie's story becomes a testament to the power of self-awareness, resilience, and the beauty of a love that thrives on authenticity, trust and emotional connection.

Her journey serves as a reminder that through personal growth, facing and questioning our fears, and emotional exploration, we can find the secure and meaningful connections that we all crave, creating a life filled with love, joy, and a sense of purpose.

CELESTE | THE SECURELY ATTACHED

Chapter 1 | The Secure Foundation

Meet Celeste, a woman who exudes confidence, empathy, and a deep sense of security in her relationships. From an early age, she experienced consistent care and love from her caregivers, laying the foundation for a secure attachment style. As she grew into adulthood, this secure attachment became the cornerstone of her romantic relationships.

Celeste approaches love with an open heart and a genuine belief in the goodness of others. Her secure attachment style allows her to trust and be trusted, fostering a sense of emotional intimacy and connection with her partners. She values open communication and emotional honesty, building relationships on a strong and stable foundation.

She exudes confidence, empathy, and a deep sense of security in her relationships. From an early age, she experienced consistent care and love from her caregivers, laying the foundation for a secure attachment style. As she grew into adulthood, this secure attachment became the cornerstone of her romantic relationships.

In a quaint suburban neighborhood, Celeste's childhood was a tapestry of love, warmth, and care. From the very beginning, she was surrounded by caregivers who provided consistent love and attention, nurturing a deep sense of security within her. Her parents, in particular, were a constant source of affection and support, always present to celebrate her victories and comfort her during difficult times.

This foundation of love and secure attachment style was the fertile ground from which Celeste's confidence and empathy would bloom. As she grew into adulthood, she carried the lessons of trust and emotional stability with her, allowing them to become the cornerstone of her romantic relationships.

Celeste's first experiences of love and security instilled in her a belief that people were inherently good and that love was a force of positivity and joy. She approached the world with an open heart, ever ready to offer a listening ear, a kind word, or a supportive hand to those around her.

In her teenage years, Celeste's friendships became a testament to her ability to foster emotional intimacy and connection. Her friends sought solace and guidance in her empathetic nature, knowing that they could confide in her without fear of judgment.

As she ventured into the world of romantic relationships, Celeste brought with her the emotional intelligence and understanding that had defined her childhood and adolescence. Her partners were drawn to her warmth and ability to create a safe space for vulnerability.

Celeste's secure attachment style allowed her to navigate the ups and downs of romantic love with a sense of grace and resilience. She knew that love was not always smooth sailing, but she approached challenges with an unwavering belief that honest communication and emotional support could overcome any obstacle.

Her romantic partners found solace in the emotional security that Celeste provided. They knew that they could trust her wholeheartedly and be their authentic selves, without fear of rejection or abandonment. This secure attachment style became the bedrock upon which their relationships could flourish.

Celeste's confidence in love extended beyond her own relationships. As a friend, confidant, and partner, she inspired those around her to believe in the power of secure attachment and emotional connection. Her presence was a beacon of stability and understanding in a world that often felt uncertain and chaotic.

With each romantic connection she formed, Celeste's capacity for love and empathy grew stronger. She continued to cherish the lessons of her childhood, valuing the importance of consistent care and emotional support in nurturing love.

As she looked back on her life, Celeste felt grateful for the secure attachment style that had been gifted to her through her upbringing. It had not shielded her from challenges, but it had given her the tools to face them with courage and resilience.

In the chapters to come, we will follow Celeste's journey of love and growth as she embraces the beauty of emotional intimacy and continues to cherish the secure attachment that has guided her throughout her life.

Her story will be a testament to the transformative power of consistent care and love, reminding us all that the foundation of love we build in our formative years can shape the trajectory of our relationships and our capacity for empathy and understanding.

Chapter 2 | Embracing Vulnerability

In her romantic relationships, Celeste shows a remarkable ability to embrace vulnerability. She recognizes that opening herself up to her partners is a sign of strength, not weakness. With honesty and authenticity, she communicates her needs, fears, and desires, fostering an atmosphere of emotional safety and intimacy in her relationships.

Her partners find comfort in knowing that they can be themselves with Celeste, free from judgment or criticism. Through her secure attachment, she helps her partners feel accepted and cherished for who they truly are.

In the cozy ambiance of a candlelit dinner, Celeste sat across from her partner, Ethan, a gentle smile gracing her lips. As they savored each other's company, a moment of vulnerability presented itself, and Celeste decided to seize it.

Taking a deep breath, Celeste gently set her fork aside and locked her gaze with Ethan. "There's something I've been wanting to talk about," she began, her voice soft and steady. "I've been thinking about how important it is for us to be open and honest with each other. So, I want to share something that's been on my mind lately."

Ethan nodded, his eyes reflecting the same sense of warmth and care that Celeste had shown him countless times before. "Of course, Celeste. You can always talk to me about anything. "Celeste felt a wave of comfort wash over her, knowing she had a partner who truly valued her vulnerability.

She continued, "You see, sometimes I have this fear that I might say or do something that could push you away. It's like this nagging worry that I might lose you." Alex reached across the table, gently taking her hand in his. "Celeste, you don't have to fear losing me. I'm right here, and I'm not going anywhere," he reassured her. "And I'm so glad you shared this with me. It shows how much you trust me, and I want you to know that I cherish that trust."

Celeste's heart swelled with gratitude for Ethan's understanding and support. "Thank you," she whispered, a glimmer of tears in her eyes. "It means a lot to me to have a partner like you who listens and accepts me as I am."

In that tender moment of vulnerability, Celeste and Ethan deepened their emotional connection. By sharing her fears and insecurities, Celeste had opened the door to greater intimacy and understanding in their relationship. Instead of being met with judgment or criticism, she found acceptance and comfort in Ethan's response.

Celeste's remarkable ability to embrace vulnerability extended to all her romantic relationships. She understood that opening herself up to her partners was not a sign of weakness, but rather a display of strength and trust. By communicating her needs, fears, and desires honestly and authentically, she fostered an atmosphere of emotional safety and intimacy.

Her partners found solace in the knowledge that they could be themselves with Celeste, without fear of judgment or rejection. They knew that she would listen with empathy and compassion, offering her support and love without conditions.

Through her secure attachment style, Celeste helped her partners feel accepted and cherished for who they truly were. She understood that everyone had their vulnerabilities and insecurities, and she celebrated the uniqueness of each individual.

In return, her partners reciprocated by opening up and allowing themselves to be vulnerable with her. They knew that vulnerability was a two-way street, and Celeste had shown them that it was a powerful tool for building emotional intimacy and trust.

With each relationship she formed, Celeste's capacity for empathy and understanding grew stronger. She cherished the privilege of being a safe space for her partners, knowing that their emotional well-being was just as important as her own.

Celeste's journey of embracing vulnerability was a testament to the power of emotional authenticity in romantic relationships. It taught her that vulnerability was not a weakness to be hidden but a strength to be celebrated.

Chapter 3 | Nurturing Emotional Intimacy

Celeste cherishes emotional intimacy in her romantic relationships. She understands that true connection goes beyond physical attraction, and she invests time and effort in cultivating deep emotional bonds with her partners.

Her secure attachment style enables her to be attuned to her partners' needs and emotions, fostering a sense of closeness and understanding. Through her empathetic nature, Celeste creates a safe space for her partners to share their feelings and vulnerabilities, further strengthening the emotional intimacy they share. Celeste had always believed that emotional intimacy was the heart and soul of any romantic relationship. For her, it was not enough to share laughter and joy or to be physically close to her partners. True connection, she knew, went deeper than the surface.

With each romantic partner she encountered, Celeste made it her mission to cultivate emotional intimacy and create a bond that transcended the ordinary. She understood that this required time, effort, and a genuine interest in getting to know her partner on a profound level.

In the early stages of a relationship, Celeste would eagerly engage in heartfelt conversations, asking thoughtful questions and actively listening to her partner's responses. She wanted to know their dreams, their fears, and their deepest desires. Her secure attachment style allowed her to be present and attuned to their needs and emotions.

As she immersed herself in these intimate exchanges, Celeste's partners felt seen and valued in a way they hadn't experienced before. She had a way of drawing out their true selves, creating a safe space for them to share their feelings and vulnerabilities without judgment.

Through her empathetic nature, Celeste offered unwavering support to her partners. She was a source of comfort in times of distress, a sounding board for their worries and anxieties, and a cheerleader for their triumphs and achievements. Her partners knew they could trust her with their most intimate thoughts and feelings, knowing she would hold them with care and understanding.

In return, her partners felt empowered to open up and be vulnerable with her. They knew that their emotions were welcomed and embraced, creating a profound sense of closeness and trust in the relationship.

Celeste's dedication to emotional intimacy extended beyond verbal exchanges. She valued quality time spent together, where they could bask in each other's presence without distractions. Whether it was a quiet night in, enjoying a movie together, or an adventure exploring a new city, she cherished every moment of emotional connection.

In times of conflict or disagreements, Celeste approached the situation with empathy and compassion. She understood that conflicts were natural in any relationship and were opportunities for growth and understanding. Instead of avoiding or dismissing them, she encouraged open and honest communication, seeking resolution together as a team.

Her secure attachment style was a guiding light in navigating the complexities of emotional intimacy. It allowed her to be attuned to her partner's emotional cues and respond with sensitivity, fostering a sense of emotional safety and closeness.

With each romantic partner, Celeste's capacity for emotional intimacy deepened. She understood that love was not solely about grand gestures and fleeting moments of passion; it was about the enduring emotional connection that could weather the storms of life.

Her partners found solace in knowing that they had a partner who saw them, heard them, and cherished the emotional bond they shared. In Celeste's arms, they found comfort and understanding, an anchor in a chaotic world.

As Celeste continued on her journey of love and growth, she knew that emotional intimacy would always be at the heart of her relationships. She understood that it required continuous nurturing and investment, just like a delicate flower that needed care to bloom fully.

Chapter 4 | Building Trust and Security

Trust and security are paramount in Celeste's romantic relationships. Her consistent care and emotional availability help her partners feel assured that she is there for them, no matter the circumstances. She is reliable, dependable, and always willing to lend a listening ear or a helping hand.

Celeste's partners know that they can rely on her support and love, creating a sense of safety and stability in their relationships. This trust serves as the bedrock upon which their love can flourish and grow.

Trust and security were the pillars that upheld Celeste's romantic relationships. Her consistent care and emotional availability were the cornerstones upon which her partners knew they could rely. No matter the circumstances, Celeste was a steadfast presence in their lives, offering unwavering support and love.

In the ebb and flow of life, Celeste's partners found solace in her reliability and dependability. Whether they were celebrating moments of triumph or weathering challenges, they knew they could count on her to be by their side, a beacon of stability in a constantly changing world.

Celeste's secure attachment style enabled her to be attuned to her partner's needs and emotions. She had a remarkable ability to sense when her partner needed comfort, reassurance, or a listening ear. Her emotional intelligence allowed her to respond with empathy and compassion, offering her support without hesitation.

In times of joy, Celeste was the first to cheer her partner on, celebrating their accomplishments with genuine excitement and pride. She recognized that love was not just about being present in difficult times but also about sharing in the joys and successes of life.

When her partner faced challenges, Celeste provided a safe space for them to express their worries and anxieties without fear of judgment. She listened attentively, offering her perspective and insights with care and understanding. Her partners knew they could rely on her to be a confidant and advisor, guiding them through moments of uncertainty.

Through her secure attachment style, Celeste built a sense of safety and stability in her relationships. Her partners knew they could lean on her in times of need, trusting that she would be there for them, no matter the circumstances.

This bedrock of trust was the foundation upon which their love could flourish and grow. With each passing day, Celeste's partners felt more secure and emotionally connected to her, allowing their bond to deepen in profound ways.

In times of doubt or vulnerability, Celeste's partners found comfort in knowing that she was not one to waver in her support and love. They knew that her commitment to their relationship was unwavering, rooted in a genuine care and affection that was evident in every interaction they shared.

Celeste's ability to foster trust and security in her relationships was a testament to her understanding of the importance of emotional safety. She knew that vulnerability was not a weakness but a sign of strength and courage. By creating a safe space for her partners to be their authentic selves, she nurtured emotional intimacy and openness.

As her relationships continued to flourish, Celeste's partners reciprocated her trust and support. They knew that they, too, could rely on her as a source of stability and love. In this reciprocal exchange of trust, their bond grew stronger, with each partner feeling cherished and valued in a relationship built on emotional security.

Chapter 5 | Embracing & Celebrating Individuality

Celeste values individuality in both herself and her romantic partners. She understands that each person is unique, with their own dreams, aspirations, and interests. Her secure attachment allows her to embrace her partners' individuality, encouraging them to pursue their passions and grow as individuals.

She recognizes that healthy relationships thrive when both partners have the freedom to be themselves and pursue their own personal growth. Celeste celebrates her partners' achievements and supports them in their endeavors, fostering a sense of mutual respect and admiration.

Celeste had always believed that love was not about molding someone into an idealized version of a partner but celebrating the beauty of their individuality. Her secure attachment style allowed her to embrace her partners' uniqueness, recognizing that each person was on their own journey of self-discovery and growth.

As she embarked on new romantic relationships, Celeste made it a point to get to know her partners on a deep level. She asked about their dreams, aspirations, and interests, genuinely curious about what made them tick and what brought them joy.

She understood that healthy relationships thrived when both partners had the freedom to be themselves and pursue their own personal growth. Celeste encouraged her partners to follow their passions and explore their interests, offering her unwavering support along the way.

When her partner found joy in their hobbies, whether it was painting, playing an instrument, or participating in sports, Celeste was their biggest cheerleader. She celebrated their achievements and milestones, reveling in the happiness that radiated from them.

In turn, her partners felt a profound sense of acceptance and validation. They knew that they could be their authentic selves with Celeste, free from judgment or pressure to conform to societal expectations.

Celeste's ability to embrace individuality extended to her own life as well. She understood that she, too, had her dreams and passions that were independent of her romantic relationships. She continued to pursue her interests and hobbies, enriching her life and bringing her a sense of fulfillment and purpose.

As she nurtured her own growth, Celeste found that it strengthened the bond she shared with her partners. They respected her independence and admired her dedication to self-discovery and personal growth.

In times of difficulty or self-doubt, Celeste was a source of encouragement, reminding her partners of their unique strengths and capabilities. She believed in their potential and inspired them to overcome obstacles with resilience and determination.

In celebrating her partners' individuality, Celeste fostered a sense of mutual respect and admiration in her relationships. They cherished her ability to see the best in them, empowering them to be the best version of themselves.

Her secure attachment style was instrumental in this celebration of individuality. It allowed her to trust in the strength of her relationships, knowing that her partners' personal growth was not a threat to their bond but an opportunity for deeper connection.

Celeste's partners marveled at the freedom they felt in her presence. They knew that they could explore and evolve as individuals without fear of outgrowing the relationship. Her unwavering support and belief in their uniqueness created an emotional safety net that allowed them to thrive and flourish.

With each romantic connection she formed, Celeste's appreciation for individuality grew stronger. She recognized that each partner brought something unique to the relationship, enriching their bond in ways she could have never imagined.

Celeste's journey of love and growth is a reminder that love flourishes when both partners are free to be themselves, and that by encouraging each other's growth and individuality, we can create a love that is as boundless and unique as the individuals who share it.

Chapter 6 | Conflict Resolution with Compassion

Like any relationship, Celeste's romantic partnerships encounter challenges and conflicts. However, her secure attachment style helps her navigate these moments with grace and compassion. She approaches conflicts with a willingness to understand her partner's perspective and find common ground.

Celeste does not shy away from difficult conversations, as she knows that open communication is essential for resolving conflicts. Through empathy and active listening, she fosters an environment of understanding and teamwork, allowing her relationships to emerge stronger after every hurdle.

Like the ebb and flow of the tide, challenges and conflicts were inevitable in Celeste's romantic relationships. However, she approached these moments with a sense of grace and compassion, guided by her secure attachment style and unwavering commitment to emotional intimacy.

When conflicts arose, Celeste didn't shy away from difficult conversations. Instead, she embraced them as opportunities for growth and understanding. She knew that open communication was essential for resolving conflicts and strengthening the bond she shared with her partner.

With a heart filled with empathy, Celeste actively listened to her partner's perspective. She put herself in their shoes, seeking to understand the emotions and experiences that shaped their point of view. This willingness to empathize created an environment of trust and vulnerability, where her partner felt safe to express their thoughts and feelings.

Through active listening, Celeste fostered a sense of understanding and teamwork in her relationships. Instead of seeking to prove her point or defend her stance, she prioritized finding common ground and a shared solution. Her partners knew that she wasn't interested in winning an argument but rather in finding a resolution that honored both of their feelings and needs.

During challenging moments, Celeste's secure attachment style provided a guiding light. It allowed her to remain emotionally present and engaged, even in times of conflict. She never resorted to avoidance or emotional distancing, recognizing that these behaviors could exacerbate the issue rather than resolve it.

Her partners found comfort in knowing that Celeste was a partner they could lean on during difficult times. They felt reassured that she wouldn't let conflicts erode the foundation of trust and love they had built together.

Celeste's commitment to open communication and understanding didn't mean that conflicts were always easily resolved. There were moments of frustration and hurt, but she approached them with a sense of humility and a willingness to take responsibility for her part in the situation.

Through her secure attachment style, Celeste demonstrated that conflicts were not threats to the relationship but opportunities for deeper emotional connection and growth. She believed that by working through challenges together, their bond could emerge even stronger.

In the aftermath of conflicts, Celeste made a conscious effort to nurture the emotional intimacy in her relationships. She prioritized acts of kindness and affection, reminding her partner of the love and care they shared. Her secure attachment allowed her to rebuild trust and emotional connection, creating a stronger and more resilient relationship.

With each conflict they navigated together, Celeste's relationships became a testament to the power of open communication, empathy, and understanding. She knew that conflicts were not signs of a failing relationship, but natural occurrences in the journey of love.

Her secure attachment style served as a guiding compass, allowing her to navigate the storms with grace and compassion. Through her actions and words, she showed her partners that their emotional well-being and the health of their relationship were of utmost importance to her.

Her story will be a reminder that conflicts are opportunities for emotional intimacy and understanding, and that by fostering open communication and empathy, we can overcome hurdles and emerge with a love that is even more profound and resilient.

Chapter 7 | Savoring the Present Moment

Celeste embraces the beauty of the present moment in her romantic relationships. Her secure attachment style allows her to live in the present without dwelling on past insecurities or future uncertainties. She values the time she spends with her partners and makes the most of every precious moment.

By savoring the present, Celeste experiences a deep appreciation for the love and connection she shares with her partners. She is mindful of the little gestures of affection and the shared laughter that make their relationships so special.

For Celeste, the beauty of love lay not in reminiscing about the past or anxiously anticipating the future but in savoring the present moment with her partners. Her secure attachment style allowed her to live in the now, free from the shackles of past insecurities or future uncertainties.

When she was with her partners, Celeste was fully present, immersing herself in every shared experience, no matter how big or small. From romantic dinners to lazy Sunday mornings, she valued every moment spent together, recognizing that love was a tapestry woven with the threads of present connections.

She had learned to let go of past hurts and insecurities, understanding that dwelling on them only hindered the potential for joy and growth in her relationships. Instead, she chose to focus on the present, embracing the love and connection she shared with her partners.

Celeste's ability to be present allowed her to be mindful of the little gestures of affection that made their relationships special. A gentle touch, a knowing smile, or a heartfelt compliment—she cherished each expression of love, recognizing that it was these small moments that added up to the grand tapestry of their love story.

In the hurried pace of modern life, Celeste's dedication to cherishing the present was a breath of fresh air for her partners. They felt seen and appreciated, knowing that when they were together, nothing else mattered but the bond they shared.

Her partners found solace in knowing that Celeste was fully engaged in their relationship, not distracted by past grievances or future uncertainties. They knew that when they were together, they had her undivided attention and affection.

Through her secure attachment style, Celeste experienced a deep appreciation for the love and connection she shared with her partners. She understood that love was not just about grand gestures or extravagant expressions but about the everyday moments of connection and intimacy.

With each passing day, Celeste's love for her partners grew deeper. She learned to relish the little things—the inside jokes, the shared hobbies, and the quiet moments of contentment—that brought joy and meaning to their relationship.

In the fast-paced world, Celeste's dedication to cherishing the present was a powerful reminder of the beauty of simplicity and connection. She knew that life was too short to get lost in what had been or what might be; the true essence of love lay in the here and now.

As she continued to embrace the present, Celeste's relationships thrived with a sense of vitality and enthusiasm. She understood that the key to a lasting and fulfilling love was to cherish the beauty of every moment shared with her partner.

In the chapters to come, we will continue to follow Celeste's journey of love and growth as she navigates the complexities of cherishing the present in her relationships. Her story will be a testament to the power of living in the now, finding joy in the everyday moments, and embracing the love and connection that blossom in the present.

Chapter 8 | Navigating Change and Growth

As life brings new challenges and opportunities, Celeste navigates change and growth with a sense of adaptability and positivity. Her secure attachment style enables her to embrace change as a natural part of life's journey, fostering resilience and strength in her relationships.

With Celeste by their side, her partners feel encouraged to embrace change and pursue personal growth. She supports them as they embark on new paths, understanding that growth as individuals only enriches their bond as a couple.

As life unfolded with its ever-changing landscape, Celeste approached each new challenge and opportunity with a sense of adaptability and positivity. Her secure attachment style allowed her to navigate change as a natural part of life's journey, fostering resilience and strength in her relationships.

Celeste didn't resist or fear the unknown. Instead, she welcomed it as an opportunity for growth and self-discovery. She understood that life was a constant evolution, and embracing change was essential for personal development and emotional well-being.

With an open heart and an optimistic spirit, Celeste encouraged her partners to embrace change and pursue personal growth. She knew that as they evolved as individuals, their bond as a couple would be enriched, deepening the emotional connection they shared.

When her partners faced new opportunities or challenges, Celeste offered her unwavering support. Whether it was a career change, a new hobby, or a shift in personal goals, she was their biggest cheerleader, reminding them that she believed in their abilities and potential.

Her secure attachment style allowed her to hold space for her partners as they navigated change. She recognized that vulnerability and uncertainty were natural during times of transition, and she provided a safe space for them to express their feelings and fears without judgment.

With Celeste by their side, her partners felt encouraged and empowered to embrace change and pursue personal growth. They knew that they didn't have to face life's challenges alone, as they had a partner who would be there to support and uplift them every step of the way.

As they embarked on new paths, Celeste's admiration and respect for her partners grew. She celebrated their achievements and milestones, recognizing the courage and dedication it took to navigate change and pursue personal growth.

Through her secure attachment style, Celeste fostered a sense of stability and security in her relationships, even during times of change. Her partners knew that she was a constant source of support and love, a rock they could lean on in times of uncertainty.

In turn, her partners' growth and personal development inspired Celeste to continue on her own journey of self-discovery. She knew that personal growth was not limited to any specific phase of life; it was a continuous process that enriched every aspect of life.

As they evolved as individuals, Celeste's relationships flourished with a deeper sense of intimacy and connection. They appreciated the space she provided for them to grow and change, knowing that their bond was built on a foundation of trust and mutual respect.

Her story will be a reminder that with an adaptable and positive outlook, we can face life's challenges with strength and resilience, and that by embracing change, we open ourselves up to the endless possibilities of growth and love.

Chapter 9 | Celebrating Love and Connection

For Celeste, love is a celebration of connection and understanding. Her secure attachment style allows her to cherish the love she shares with her partners, knowing that it is based on mutual trust, respect, and emotional intimacy.

She revels in the joy of simple moments shared with her partners, whether it's a quiet evening at home or an adventurous trip together. Celeste understands that the true essence of love lies in the small, meaningful moments that they create together.

For Celeste, love was not just a fleeting emotion but a celebration of connection and understanding. Her secure attachment style allowed her to cherish the love she shared with her partners, knowing that it was based on a foundation of mutual trust, respect, and emotional intimacy.

In the midst of life's chaotic dance, Celeste found joy in the simple moments shared with her partners. Whether it was a quiet evening at home, snuggled up together on the couch, or an adventurous trip to a new destination, she understood that love was about savoring every moment they created together.

Celeste had learned that the true essence of love lay not in grand gestures or extravagant displays but in the small, meaningful moments of connection they shared. A shared laugh, a gentle touch, or a heartfelt conversation— these were the moments that brought joy and depth to their relationship.

With her secure attachment style, Celeste was fully present in these precious moments. She immersed herself in the emotions and experiences, cherishing the love they shared with a heart filled with gratitude and contentment.

In the quiet moments, Celeste reveled in the comfort and familiarity of her partner's presence. She knew that the strength of their emotional bond was what made these moments so special, allowing them to feel at home in each other's arms.

During their adventures together, Celeste embraced the exhilaration of exploring new places and trying new experiences. She understood that love was not just about being comfortable in each other's company but also about supporting and encouraging each other to grow and expand their horizons.

As they navigated life's journey hand in hand, Celeste and her partners found joy in celebrating each other's successes and triumphs. Whether it was a personal achievement or a collective milestone, they knew that they could rely on each other to be their biggest cheerleader.

Celeste's ability to find joy in the simple moments and celebrate the connection she shared with her partners was a testament to her understanding of the true essence of love. She knew that love was not about possessing or controlling someone but about embracing the beauty of their unique souls.

Through her secure attachment style, Celeste nurtured a sense of emotional intimacy in her relationships. She valued open communication and vulnerability, knowing that it was through these channels that their bond would continue to deepen and grow.

In the journey of love, Celeste reveled in the moments of connection and understanding, cherishing the beauty of their shared experiences. She knew that love was not a destination but a continuous celebration of the emotional connection they fostered together.

With each passing day, Celeste's love for her partners grew stronger. She understood that love was not just an emotion but a conscious choice to celebrate the beauty of their relationship, embracing both the highs and the lows with a heart full of love and gratitude.

Chapter 10 | A Love That Endures

As Celeste's romantic journey unfolds, her secure attachment style continues to shape her relationships. Her ability to embrace vulnerability, nurture emotional intimacy, and build trust and security lays the groundwork for a love that endures the test of time.

With Celeste's secure attachment style as their anchor, her partners find comfort in knowing that they have a love that is steadfast and enduring. As she continues to embrace her true self and cherish the uniqueness of her partners, Celeste's journey of love and growth becomes an inspiring testament to the power of secure attachment in building lasting and fulfilling relationships.

As Celeste's romantic journey continued to unfold, her secure attachment style remained the guiding force that shaped her relationships. With each passing chapter, she deepened her understanding of love, embracing vulnerability, nurturing emotional intimacy, and building trust and security with her partners.

Celeste's ability to embrace vulnerability allowed her to be her authentic self in her relationships. She understood that love required openness and honesty, and she never shied away from expressing her true feelings and emotions. This vulnerability created a space for her partners to do the same, fostering a deep sense of emotional intimacy in their connection.

Through her secure attachment style, Celeste continued to prioritize open communication and empathy in her relationships. She remained attuned to her partner's needs and emotions, offering unwavering support and understanding in times of both joy and difficulty.

As her relationships evolved, Celeste's partners found comfort in knowing that they had a love that was steadfast and enduring. They cherished the emotional security she provided, knowing that they could count on her to be there through life's highs and lows.

Celeste's secure attachment style allowed her to build trust and security in her relationships. Her partners knew that they could rely on her to be consistent and emotionally available, creating a sense of safety that allowed their love to flourish.

Her ability to celebrate the uniqueness of her partners was a testament to her understanding that love was not about finding someone to complete her but about cherishing the individuality and differences that enriched their relationship.

With each partner, Celeste continued to learn and grow, embracing the joys and challenges that came with love. She understood that no relationship was perfect, but with open hearts and a commitment to emotional intimacy, love could endure and thrive.

As Celeste embraced her true self and allowed her secure attachment style to anchor her relationships, her journey of love and growth became an inspiring testament to the power of secure attachment in building lasting and fulfilling partnerships.

Her story served as a reminder that love was not just a fleeting emotion but a conscious choice to nurture and cherish the emotional connection shared with a partner. With each chapter, Celeste's relationships continued to evolve and deepen, guided by the unwavering commitment to emotional intimacy and vulnerability.

In the end, Celeste's journey of love and growth was a testament to the power of secure attachment in building enduring and meaningful relationships. Her story offered hope and inspiration, showing that love was a journey of self-discovery, emotional connection, and the celebration of each unique and beautiful soul that came into her life.

CONCLUSION

As we conclude this exploration into the intricate dance of love and attachment, I hope you have found a deeper understanding of not only the four attachment styles that shape our relationships but also the beautiful complexity of human emotions and challenges. Through these pages, we have delved into the patterns that govern our intimate connections, unearthing the roots of our desires, fears, and hopes; and how they are connected to the early years of childhood.

This journey is not meant to confine you within the bounds of a single attachment style, but rather to empower you with the knowledge to recognize, reflect upon, and perhaps even transform your approach to love. Just as we are not static beings, our attachment styles can evolve as we gain insight and work towards greater emotional health and more secure connections.

As you close this book and step back into the reality of your own life, take with you the awareness that change is possible. Whether you resonate with the secure embrace, the anxious yearning, the avoidant independence, or the fluctuating currents of the disorganized style, you possess the remarkable capacity to nurture and heal your relationships.

Embrace the wisdom gained from understanding attachment styles and apply it to your interactions. Cultivate self-awareness and empathy, both for yourself and for your partners. Remember that the path to secure attachment is paved with patience, self-compassion, commitment, perseverance through the process, and open communication.

My hope for you is that you embark on a journey of love that is guided by authenticity, vulnerability, openness, and growth. Relationships are the canvas upon which we paint our lives, and each stroke contributes to the masterpiece we create.

Your story is still being written, and as you turn these final pages, let them mark the beginning of a new chapter — an opportunity to forge connections that are rooted in understanding, respect, and profound affection.

The road ahead may hold its challenges, but armed with the insights you've gained, you have the potential to navigate them with grace and resilience. Believe in your capacity to love and be loved, to mend what is broken, and to thrive amidst the intricate interplay of attachment challenges.

As you continue your journey, remember to embrace the boundless realm of love with a heart that is both wiser and more compassionate. Your journey continues, and the pages you write hold the promise of a story enriched by the power to change, where love knows no bounds and the human spirit soars.